Unleash the WINNER *Within You*

A Success Game Plan for Business, Leadership and Life

Honor your inner winner!

Coach W—

COACH SHERRY M. WINN

DEDICATION

This book is dedicated to my parents, Darlene and Clarence. You gave me the strength, courage and the determination to reach the seemingly impossible. You pushed me out of my comfort zone, believed in my talents, and presented me with the tools to create the world I desired. You provided me with the lessons I needed but not necessarily wanted. Thank you both for loving me as I am. I am forever grateful.

THE IDEAL SPEAKER FOR YOUR NEXT EVENT!

Any organization that wants to invigorate, stimulate and rejuvenate their team members needs to hire Coach Winn for a keynote and/or seminar training!!

To Contact or Book Coach Winn to Speak:
Ucancreatesuccess LLC
1193 Nye Road, Fishtail, MT 59028
304-380-4398

coachwinn@coachwinnspeaks.com
www.coachwinnspeaks.com
www.facebook.com/coachwinnspeaks
www.twitter.com/coachwinnspeaks

BOOK TESTIMONIES FOR UNLEASH THE WINNER

"This book is a powerful mission statement for those individuals who know the key to success is knowledge. Coach Winn shares her WIN philosophy which helped her become a two-time Olympian and a national championship coach. She gives you a road map to take yourself from ordinary to extraordinary."

— **Eldonna Lewis Fernandez, MSgt USAF Retired**
Award Winning Speaker, Award Winning Author

"Unleash the Winner shows Sherry's inspirational transformation from the dark times and challenges that she overcame and the lessons she learned from it. I can see that anyone who commits to using the WIN Philosophy and WINNER Principles will be able to grow, improve and become successful. This is a must read for anyone who has challenges and troubled times and needs help to Win!"

— **Dr. Michael Kurland, Ed.D**
Author of "The Magical Peach Twins Save Breakfast,"
CEO of Kurland Education Inc.
Award winning Director/Producer
Top 5% Publishing Kickstarter Fundraiser

"There is a winner inside of you, and The Win Philosophy provides you a blueprint for letting your brightness shine in the world. Learn from an expert, and let proven winner Sherry Winn coach you to success. Her clarity and ability to reach all people with her positive and uplifting message is reflected on every page. After you have spent time with this book, internalizing Sherry's ideas and insights, you will be changed in a positive way for the rest of your life."

— **Dr. Danny Brassell, "America's Leading Reading**
Ambassador," Founder of "The Lazy Readers'
Book Club"

"Sherry's writings espouse wisdom and honesty. Her personal growth and transformation are an inspiration. In her book, she uses her life lessons as cornerstones for change, and guides the reader to new insights and perspectives. I encourage everyone to delve into to this book!"

> — **Dr. Pam Winn, Ed.D, Tarleton State University, Associate Professor/NCELP Director/Master's Coordinator/ESP Director**

"While many talk about winning, Sherry brings a fresh understanding for anyone to achieve great accomplishments with her WIN philosophy. As someone who has been there, done it and is still doing it, Sherry's insights and abilities will unleash your unlimited potential. *Unleash The Winner* is a must read for anyone who is ready to embrace their destiny and stand in their "WINNERS CIRCLE"!"

> — **Gary Barnes "America's Traction Coach"**
> **Author- International Speaker- High Performance Business & Sales Coach**

"Crafted from transformational lessons learned on her life's journey, Sherry's WIN Philosophy offers durable, empowering principles for personal growth and meaningful living. Insightful, inspirational, and life-affirming, *Unleash the Winner Within You* provides a pathway for positive change, personal integrity and success."

> — **Reita Clanton, 1984 Olympian, 1996 Assistant Olympic Coach, Director of Performance Optimization, Auburn University School of Kinesiology**

"As someone who has faced multiple adversities by suffering two brain injuries within 40 days, I understand that having an amazing coach and game plan is essential for success. National Championship Coach and Olympian, Sherry Winn's book and her WIN philosophy provide that HELPful game plan. She is the force behind a raw and real wake up call for anyone who wants to be a WINNER in business or in life."

— Heather Walker, Author of "Don't Give Up, Get Up" and the HELPful Philosophy, Top Selling Author, Nationally Recognized Speaker, and Leading Trainer

"Because you want to learn from an inspiring and successful coach, you MUST READ this book. Coach Winn has taken situations, events, and experiences from her life and developed a powerful WIN Philosophy which has worked for her and will work for you. This philosophy propelled her forward to becoming a two time Olympian and led to her success with championship teams. You too have the ability to follow her WIN philosophy and achieve success with a positive perspective. Use the WIN philosophy in YOUR life and join others who are already applying the WIN philosophy and experiencing success in their lives!"

— Lila M Larson, Award winning National trainer, Consultant, Speaker, Author of: "*Small Business BIG GROWTH*"

"The Olympic motto is Citius, Altius, Fortius. The English translation is Swifter, Higher, Stronger. As Olympic competitors we strive to achieve the highest level of athletic performance. Becoming an Olympian is one of the most challenging endeavors any athlete can undertake. If you want to be successful, if you commit to be successful, read this book and learn from it. In today's fast paced world of reaching the highest level of achievement, this book will help you "restart" your approach and take you to heights you could only dream of!"

— **Cindy Stinger, Manager, United States Olympians and Paralympians Association, United States Olympic Committee, 1984, 1988, 1992 U.S. Olympic Team**

ABOUT COACH SHERRY WINN

Coach Sherry Winn is an in-demand motivational speaker, a leading success coach and seminar trainer, a two-time Olympian, a national championship basketball coach, and an Amazon best seller. She has written five books including, *"Unleash the Winner within You: A Success Game Plan for Business, Leadership and Life."* Thousands, from small business owners to athletic coaches to corporate executives, have enjoyed Coach Winn's powerful interactive and humorous WINNING presentations.

With over 34 years of practicing leadership as an elite athlete and collegiate basketball coach, Sherry is an expert on coaching leaders and team members to championship status. She has successfully taken people beyond their levels of comfort to "WIN" against competitors who were superior in talent, facilities and financial budgets. Through her WIN Philosophy™ and WINNER Principles™, she teaches leaders and team members to be victorious even when the odds appear to be insurmountable.

A recognized authority on leadership and team development, Coach Winn shares with you the WINNER Principles which will enable you to rejuvenate, invigorate and stimulate you and your team members to become agents of change.

Audiences rave about Coach Winn's ability to enthusiastically deliver messages woven into humorous stories which are applicable for individuals within all levels of organizations. A passionate, sought-after author, speaker and business consultant, Coach Winn is characterized by friends, colleagues and clients as one of the most benevolent, perceptive and influential individuals in the business today.

To find out more about Coach Winn's seminars, books, trainings, and coaching, or to inquire about Coach Winn's availability to speak, you can contact her office at:

www.CoachWinnSpeaks.com

Contents

INTRODUCTION

ACQUIRING THE RIGHT TOOLS

"The winner's edge is not in a gifted birth, a high IQ,
or in talent. The winner's edge is all in the attitude,
not aptitude. Attitude is the criterion for success."
—**Denis Waitley**

You might be the person who knows you are a winner and has always felt that way, but has recently been challenged and has lost the winning edge. You might be one of those people who subscribe to the theory there are winners and losers in life, and you happen to be one of the losers. Perhaps you are the person who believes you can be a winner, but you don't yet have the right formula. Or maybe you already are a winner and know the secret formula, which is why you are reading another book to keep you motivated to stay in the winner's circle.

It doesn't matter where you are in your thought process, today is the day you will learn or relearn the formula behind winning and how you can keep winning throughout your life.

In order to unleash the winner within you, the key ingredient is having the right tool.

Have you ever tried to hammer a nail into the wall with a pair of pliers? You probably missed the head of the nail a few times, hit your finger, and cursed at the time it was taking you. You eventually got the nail into the wall, but it wasn't an easy process. It would have been easier with a hammer. This is why you want to learn the proper tools to be successful in life. You can skip the pain, the heartache, the cursing and the hours of wrangling if you possess the right toolset.

Why am I the person who can provide you with the right tools? I've experienced both successes and failures, and have responded to the failures by growing and evolving to become even more successful. I've made some huge strides in my life:

- From the shadows of depression to the glow of optimism.
- From chronic pain to better health and vitality.
- From collegiate bench substitute to two-time Olympian.
- From termination from my first coaching job to national coach of the year.

During all those challenging times, I had doubts I could take the next step. When I was younger, my insecure voice was much louder and I almost succumbed to it. I spent 12 years fighting suicidal thoughts—those were the thoughts of a woman who didn't believe she had choices. I didn't have the right tools to help me get beyond my negative thoughts.

What happens when you hit your wall of doubts? Do you know you have choices? You can listen to the inner voice which likes to tell you that you can't, or you can choose to concentrate on finding ways you can. All of us have both voices. What separates those who succeed from those who fail is decided by what voice they empower.

We all possess equal ability to make choices. We might not have the same talents, the same emotional or social I.Q., the same financial backgrounds, or the same support systems, but we all have the ability to determine what we think. It is our thoughts which separate us. It is our thoughts which determine our future, not some magical wand or fate or inheritance. It is us.

In the first chapter, you will discover the **WIN** Philosophy.™

This is the philosophy which helped me become a two-time Olympian, overcome chronic pain, and coach a national championship team.

1. <u>Widen the Separator Gap</u>. The separator is defined as the person who goes the extra mile, who does the things nobody else is willing to do, and who does whatever it takes to reach her goals.

2. <u>Identify "I AM" as Your Power Words</u>. "I AM" are the two most powerful words in the universe. Those are the words that create your future and determine who you become.

3. <u>Navigate your success</u>. You and only you are in charge of your success. Once you take responsibility for your success and look for solutions, you will find them.

After being introduced to the **WIN** Philosophy, ™ you will further your ability to succeed through the **WINNER** Principles. ™ These principles will guide you through the WIN philosophy and help you reconnect with the miracle you are.

1. Welcome Your Challenges. Learn to look for the gems hidden within your challenges which provide you the opportunity for growth.

2. Improve Your Communication Skills. Your internal language establishes how you view yourself which in turn determines how you communicate with others.

3. Nourish Yourself. The key to unlocking your power for sharing your gifts with others is to first nourish yourself. Nobody else can nourish you as much as you can nourish yourself.

4. Nurture Your Relationships. Your relationships determine your financial possibilities, your social activities, and your personal connections. How you nurture your relationships directly affects your happiness and success.

5. Expect The Best. We are the reflection of who we think we are. When we expect the best we are more likely to receive it.

6. Recover From Your Past. We think our past governs who we become and it can, or we can choose an alternate path. We don't have to live who we once were; we can choose to become who we want to be.

This book is a road map for you to embark on a journey to re-remember the dreams you had as a young child and to know all things are possible. Your job is to connect with the force you were meant to be and allow yourself to become your greatest achievement.

CHAPTER ONE

THE WIN
PHILOSOPHY

WIDEN THE SEPARATOR GAP

Kevin Eastman, assistant coach of the Los Angeles Clippers, likes to define the "separators" as the characteristics that separate you from the average. Everyone dreams. What separates you from everyone else with a dream? The separator has the ability to take action until that dream is brought into reality.

People like to make bucket lists and wish lists and imagine the day they win the lottery but then stop at the dreaming phase. They have a million reasons why they don't have what they want in life, and instead of taking action, they watch from the sidelines, angry that someone else is living their dream.

When you are willing to do whatever it takes to make your dream a reality, you become a separator. You separate yourself from those who merely want to achieve. <u>Achievers are believers and believers are achievers, but dreamers aren't always performers.</u>

Jim Rohn, a man who took himself from rags to riches and became an inspiration to millions of people, said, "If you are not willing to risk the unusual, you will have to settle for the ordinary." Many people are afraid to reach out and risk the extra work, the reproach of friends and family, and the potential for failure. They become watchers and not doers.

If you want to WIN, to experience what other people feel is impossible, you become a separator. You teach yourself how to be unique. You go beyond the extra mile. You do things that no one else is willing to do.

When I decided to be an Olympian, I didn't just utter the words, I committed to the work. I was determined to be the first athlete in the gym and the last athlete to leave the gym. I decided that while other players were talking and goofing off, I would work. I would give more effort than anybody else on the team, and I would never give less than 100%. If I walked off the court knowing I had more inside me to give, I had failed.

I held myself to a standard few athletes could maintain, **but that was the point.** I didn't want to be like everybody else. I wanted to live my dream and not just have a fantasy in my head. I wasn't the strongest, fastest, quickest or most powerful athlete on the team. In fact, many players on my teams had as much athletic talent, but none of them had my commitment.

My teammates could have done the same things I did, but they weren't willing to be a separator.

Yet I didn't have all the answers to the equation, and I failed miserably many times because I didn't know the power of my thoughts. If I had known how to use my mind and not just my body, the road to winning would have been much shorter. I didn't have all of the right tools, but the one tool I possessed was the commitment to work harder than anyone else.

CHARACTER DRIVES THE SEPARATION

You can fantasize all you want, but to live your dream you have to possess the faith it will happen. Faith is tied directly to character. If you don't believe you deserve something, you will talk yourself out of it. You don't get what you want; you get who you are.

Do you give yourself enough credit? Or do you define yourself by your limitations and what you have not achieved? If you don't see greatness inside yourself, you can't go forward. *Your definition determines your ambition.* Think about it. However you define yourself determines how hard you are going to work, what your attitude is, and how long you will persist before you desist.

How do you define your character? Your character is the piece of you behind the commitment, the way you see yourself when no one is looking. Your character is the answer that allows you to believe "you can."

It is not enough to work harder than anybody else; you have to be willing to study, listen and be coachable. I studied the game of basketball as if it was the road map to happiness. What I failed to do was to study how to become a better person. This lack of awareness built roadblocks rather than bridges to my goals.

One of the roadblocks was the disillusionment of abandonment. I rarely got into trouble in junior high or high school, but when my parents hit a crisis with their marriage, I tumbled through the disillusionment I had been abandoned. I took their crisis personally and thought I was unlovable. The more they struggled and couldn't see my needs, the more I tumbled into disillusionment. My belief I was unlovable and unworthy grew until I searched for ways to destroy myself. I drank, cursed, used people to make me feel better, and found many ways to throw hatred upon myself.

I defined myself in ways which hindered success.

I didn't know my character hindered my progress. I didn't know that I wouldn't get what I wanted by being angry, insecure, fearful, jealous, and unconfident. Instead of working on the inside of me, I pushed my physical body to the limits. I was using pliers to drive the nail in the wall. I needed a better tool and did not know it. *In order to get what you want, you have to be willing to change who you are.* If you are not willing to change, you keep doing the wrong things over and over, and you just get better at getting worse.

If you are willing to be a separator, you go beyond the physical. While working longer and harder than most people will find you some success, you will also wake up one day to discover that your family has moved on, your friends have deserted you, and your health is failing. There is a better way which requires internal as well as external tools, and you still have to be willing to do the work.

PASSION ENABLES THE SEPARATION TO GROW

In *Think and Grow Rich*, Napoleon Hill said, "There is one quality which one must possess to win, and that is definiteness of purpose, the knowledge of what one wants, and a burning desire to possess it." The **burning desire or passion** is what keeps one moving forward when others stop at the first obstacle.

One of the qualities that separate winners is this burning desire to do, have or be. Wanting something is not enough: Winners are obsessed. Mere wanting does not get you past the fatigue, the injury, the illness, the naysayer, the lack of funds, the failures, the misery, the doubts, the anxieties or the unknown. You may have good intentions when you start your journey toward success, only to have your intentions drowned by failure.

How driven are you? Do you have enough zeal to sustain you when you don't reach your goals within six months, a year or three years?

Emotions are at the hub of personal inspiration—they provide the force and the power behind your will and actions. When your passions are triggered, you tap into astonishing motivational muscle. This muscle can push you beyond the obstacles in your path.

As a basketball coach I recruited players who showed heart. I wanted players who would do anything to win. When I saw a player dive into the bleachers, jump on top of an opponent to tie up a loose ball, or sprint for the defensive stop when it seemed the basket was inevitable, I wanted to sign her. These were the players who would be the nucleus of the team. These were the players who would carry us when the shooter went into a slump or the star wasn't in full form. These players would find a way to win when winning seemed out of reach.

The problem was that these players were rare. They were gems and every coach who knew how to win wanted them. My opposing coaches knew like I did that one player with heart could carry a team on her shoulders. Because that player exuded enthusiasm every day, she was contagious. She made others better through her burning desire to win.

Your heart should be at the center of your goals. <u>When you are fully invested in what you want, you see no other option but to sustain effort until you reach your goals</u>. Burning desire isn't a given; it is a separator.

YOUR MUSE AS A SEPARATOR

*"Instead of discussing with myself every morning whether
I feel inspired or not, I step into my office every day at nine
sharp, open the window and politely ask the muse to enter
and kiss me. Sometimes she comes in, more often she does
not. But she can never claim that she hasn't
found me waiting in the right place."*
— Peter Prange

Some people wait for inspiration. They believe inspiration will hit them on the head or knock the wind out of them. They wait and wait. They think their muse arrives on its own time table. They have no control over whether or not they are inspired.

The people who are separators don't wait; they create their own inspiration. They find ways every day to inspire themselves toward their goals. They wake up with a plan to keep themselves motivated, and then they walk through that plan and believe that it works.

In the fall of 2013, I coached a young man, Justin, who was trying to make it to the major leagues in baseball. I asked him, "What is going to separate you from the other players who are trying to make it?"

"I'm going to do the things no other player is willing to do. I'm going to spend time in the morning reading, going through my affirmations, silencing my mind and visualizing."

Justin knew his athleticism wasn't going to be enough. He also knew that other athletes would work hard, but not many of them would work the right way. After weeks of coaching, he understood what athletes meant when they said, "Winning is mostly mental."

Most athletes say this, but not many of them follow through with action steps.

The mental steps are your muse. They move you beyond the average, beyond people with dreams and beyond people with desires. Your ability to inspire yourself daily and to maintain your inspiration brings you closer to your dreams and helps you believe that you are living your dreams, even when reality tells you otherwise.

What habits do you have each morning that drive you all day long toward your goal?

Hal Elrod in his book, *The Miracle Morning: The Not-So-Obvious Secret Guaranteed to Transform Your Life Before 8 AM,* provides six practices that he uses to take his life from unfulfilled potential to extraordinary.

He defines them as Life S.A.V.E.R.S.™

1. The ability to have purposeful **SILENCE.** This silence can come in the form of prayer, meditation, deep breathing, gratitude, or reflection.

2. The determination to repeat **AFFIRMATIONS** as part of your daily routine. Affirmations allow you to design your beliefs and through constant repetition, blend your thoughts into your beliefs.

3. The capacity to use **VISUALIZATION** to see your future as happening now. Use your imagination to create pictures of positive results.

4. The resolve to **EXERCISE** as a part of your daily ritual. Exercise stimulates your emotional well-being and enables clarity of thought and more durable concentration.

5. The aptitude to **READ** to stimulate personal growth. Streamline your efforts by learning from those who have the keys to success.

6. The courage to **SCRIBE** your thoughts in a journal. The act of writing out your thoughts reveals them to you in a different way, providing valuable insight.

Every day your challenge is to be your own muse, to find the creativity that is always within you. When you look for something, you are more likely to find it. The act is as simple as it seems. The doing of it separates those who think of it as simple from those who simply do it.

MINDPOWER IS A SEPARATOR FROM WILLPOWER

When I was a teenager training for the Olympics, I believed all the old adages people told me:

✓ Where there is a will, there is a way.

✓ Willpower is the key to success.

✓ Next to courage, willpower is the most important thing.

AND these adages are all true, but what my coaches and parents didn't tell me was that willpower is not enough. It is never enough. No matter how much will you have, it will not be enough to overcome the limiting beliefs that hold you captive.

If you have the will to train hard but your subconscious mind has a different story, your willpower loses out every time. Your willpower exists in your conscious mind where it strives hard to overcome the beliefs your subconscious mind holds, and your subconscious mind holds the blueprint for how you react and believe.

Imagine you are sitting in the passenger seat. You have a map in front of you, and you read all the road signs along the highway. You point in the direction where the car should turn, but your subconscious mind is sitting behind the steering wheel and decides based on past experiences to drive straight on ahead.

You thought you were driving the car, but your subconscious mind was making the real decisions. Your conscious mind is a marvelous passenger, but your subconscious mind is the driver.

Willpower is only as strong as the beliefs you hold in the subconscious mind. Your subconscious mind absorbs all true experiential learning. While your conscious mind analyzes, rationalizes, and resolves, your subconscious mind works from habit and from thoughts that were entered by your earliest experiences.

I thought I could be an Olympic athlete. Being an Olympian was a conscious dream, wish, and goal, yet my subconscious mind believed that I wasn't good enough. No matter how hard I trained, I found ways to self-sabotage. I got injured. I drank myself silly. I yelled at my coaches. I fought with the star of the team. I excused myself for not performing at my best. All these behaviors were outcomes of my subconsious mind obeying the beliefs of my earlier experiences in life.

Willpower was not enough. Willpower got me to the banquet table but did not let me join in the feast. To align my willpower, I had to develop my mindpower. When I learned that thoughts are things and began attending to the thoughts I held—the ones telling me I wasn't tall enough, fast enough, strong enough, or talented enough—and started turning those thoughts to positive affirmations, my willpower tripled.

Willpower can get you to the brink of success, but mindpower takes you to the world of success.

SEPARATORS AIM FOR THE TOP 3%

Do you know how many high school athletes think they will play at the more prominent and better funded universities, the National Collegiate Athletic Association (NCAA) Division I universities? Do you know how many high school athletes actually receive scholarships to Division I programs?

During summer basketball camps, I asked my campers how many of them wanted to receive a collegiate basketball scholarship. Every time I asked this question, nearly every young lady raised her hand. Some of these campers raised their hands because their friends did, but many of them dreamed of becoming the next collegiate star.

According to the Georgia Career Information Center, 98 out of 100 high school athletes never play athletics at any collegiate level, and less than 1% receive a scholarship to a Division I University. Only about 3% of all male and female high school basketball players play collegiate basketball at any level, and of those players, less than 1% have the opportunity to play professionally.

No statistics are available on how many college athletes actually make it to the Olympics, but the number is far lower than the percentages who become professional athletes. I was one of the very few collegiate athletes to become an Olympian.

How did I get there? I knew I had to aim to be not just one of the best, but THE BEST.

I trained twice a day for 12 years. As a high school student I drove to school at 6:45 a.m. so I could shoot before school started. In the afternoon I trained with the team, and then practiced for an additional hour on my ball handling and passing skills. I worked out on Sundays alone for three hours perfecting my skills. During the summers I scrimmaged with the men in downtown Fort Worth where I was the only girl and usually the only white player on the court.

When I was selected for the USA Team Handball National Team, I trained twice a day all year around except on holidays. I put my college education on hold, sacrificed friendships, and moved half way across the country from my family. I did this without any compensation for my efforts. For the first year and a half of training, I worked a full time job while still maintaining a two-a-day workout schedule. I took the action most people were not willing to take.

If you want to be a WINNER, you have to think big. You have to believe you can separate yourself from the 97% of people who try to make it big, not just 97% of all people, but the 97% who are willing to try. Most people are afraid to try, and then a huge percentage of those will stop at their first failure. Your willingness to try will already take you past most people and over your first hurdles, but that is just the beginning.

To be one of the elite, to be in the top 3%, you act, think, and aim differently. You are not one of the campers who raised her hand but did not take her lessons to the next level. You have to be willing to separate yourself every single day from those who want to be in the top 3%.

Most people want something better. But as soon as they learn what it takes to be in the top 3%, they stop trying. You must be willing to believe that you are one of the elite and then take the actions that get you there.

IDENTIFY "I AM" AS POWER WORDS

Muhammad Ali said, "I am the greatest…I said that even before I knew I was." Muhammad Ali held the secret to becoming the best boxer. He told himself "I Am" as if he already was the greatest.

"I AM" are the two most powerful words in the universe, because they determine your experience. Whatever you tell yourself, you become. When you plant an apple tree in the backyard, does it grow up to be a lemon tree? No! Why not? Because whatever seeds you plant are the ones you receive. <u>The words you plant every day are growing within you</u>.

Take a moment and look back at your life. Did you think you would become a mother, a husband, a teacher, a leader, an athlete, a writer, a musician, a doctor, an artist, or an accountant? Whatever you talked about or thought about are the very things you experienced. Your thoughts were the foundation for who you became.

You might disagree. You might refer back to things you experienced that you don't consciously remember telling yourself. Perhaps you were fired from your job and you never said you desired to be terminated. You did say that you were unhappy at your job, your boss was a jerk, and you wanted to change occupations. Those were unconscious statements you made over the years, and you never connected those words with the desire to be terminated. But isn't that what you really wanted—the ability to move forward?

You might not be aware of the words you unconsciously told yourself throughout the years. Lack of awareness does not alter the outcome of your thoughts. Think about how you see yourself and how you've defined yourself. How many times have you defined yourself by words similar to these?

- I am fat.

- I am a slow learner.

- I am not good at using computers.

- I am too skinny.

- I am angry.

How many times have you repeated these thoughts to yourself? A hundred? A thousand? A million?

Those thoughts led to what you are living. If you told yourself a hundred times a day you weren't good with technology and then struggled with computers, are you surprised at the outcome?

If you told yourself you were fat for years, are you astonished that you can't lose weight no matter what you do?

If you told yourself you are angry person, are you shocked with your incapacity to reign in your anger during a conflict?

Your "I AM" statements are so powerful that they fulfill your destiny. If you want to make different life choices, tell yourself a different story. By making thought changes, you can affect your external outcomes. Start with the words, "I AM" and then complete the sentence using powerful positive descriptors. I AM:

> **amazing, magnificent, remarkable, wonderful, incredible, miraculous, astonishing, extraordinary, outstanding, noteworthy, brilliant, radiant, majestic, impressive, elegant, commanding, and awesome!**

LEARNING TO LISTEN TO YOUR "I AM" STATEMENTS

Part of the problem with understanding the two most powerful words is lack of awareness. We don't know what we don't know, and we can't learn what we need to know when we aren't aware of what it is. When you are unaware of how you use the words, "I AM," then you are in the stage of unconscious incompetence.

The four stages of learning provide a model for awareness. This model helps us understand how we move through our consciousness. We don't know that we don't know before we know what we don't know, and then we learn what we know but we still have to think about it. Finally, we come to the stage where we don't know what we know. Whew! I'm not certain I know what I wrote. That is a lot of knows. Think who you would be if you knew all those knows.

A major step to getting a winner's mindset is gaining awareness—to become aware of the things that you don't know. When you gain awareness, you begin the process of expansion. You expand from ignorance to knowing. Now some people might say that ignorance is bliss. Ignorance is bliss until you realize that ignorance does not get you what you desire, and ignorance is not a valid excuse.

When you don't know that you don't know, you are in the stage of unconscious incompetence. In 2004, I recruited a talented guard by the name of Courtney. She was fast, strong, a tremendous passer, and had moxie for the game. As a freshman her favorite phrase was, "I suck."

When she failed to understand a teaching point, she yelled, "I suck." When she missed a lay-up, she yelled, "I suck." When she blew a defensive assignment, she yelled, "I suck." She didn't understand what she was telling herself. She couldn't comprehend that what she said to herself affected the next play. The more she affirmed that she sucked, the more her play deteriorated.

How many times in a season did she plant those seeds into her brain? Hundreds of times? Yet, she expected for those seeds to be ignored and the ones she didn't plant to sprout. She didn't know how the words she planted were creating her experiences.

The second step is conscious incompetence. You arrive at the recognition of knowing what you do not know. This is scary because when you didn't know that you didn't know, you lived in blissful ignorance. Now that you are aware of how important your words are, you understand the challenge of transforming the old habits that you've acquired.

Courtney believed she played like she played—she either had a good game or a bad game. She wasn't aware of how her thoughts influenced her skills on the court.

When I taught her how powerful the words "I AM" were, she wasn't ready to take responsibility for her words. She didn't want to believe her words influenced her skills. She just wanted to play ball and ignore this mumble-jumble about affirming words. I responded by taking her out of practices and games. After two months of consistently being benched for saying, "I suck," she was forced to see how frequently she repeated this phase and to confront how it affected her play.

Even being benched was not enough consequence for Courtney. Not until she was shown on game film that her reaction to a mistake often created another mistake did she finally acknowledge her need to change.

Conscious competence: You now know what you know, but you still have to consciously think about what you are doing. After a year, Courtney learned how her words impacted her play. She understood the more she made negative statements about herself, the more poorly she performed on the court.

Courtney made a conscious effort to quit saying, "I suck," and instead say, "I'm okay." Unfortunately, the coaching staff couldn't get her to substitute a more positive phrase than "I'm okay," because she wasn't ready to believe she was more than just okay. She could only move to the level of learning that she was prepared to go.

Because Courtney had to consciously think about what she was saying before she spoke, she often regressed to her old damaging language. When she slipped, she would apologize to the team and then say her replacement phrase. She had become conscious of her language and how the words she spoke impacted her play, but her new phrase was not yet habitual.

Unconscious competence: At this phase, the learning is completed. You do not have to think about what you are doing. You don't know that you know. In other words, your learned skill is automatic.

Eventually, after Courtney practiced her "I'm Okay" phrase over and over again, she no longer had to consciously remember to say it. Her new way of thinking became that she was okay, and she became a better player. She helped our basketball team become the only team in the history of the University of Charleston to win back-to-back NCAA Regional Titles.

Unconscious competence is the state we all want to achieve in awareness. Achieving unconscious competence represents the end of a cycle and yet presents the need to begin a new cycle. The truth is that in a winner's mindset, you never reach a place where learning ends. You always want to know what you don't know. Another level of awareness awaits your discovery.

ACTION IS PREPARATION TO RECEIVE OUR "I AM" CREATIONS

Action takes place after the creation of our "I AM" thoughts. The thought of something comes before the creation of it. <u>To be a creator, we start with the thoughts of who we want to be</u>. If we neglect to tell ourselves who we want to be, we receive a default answer. The default answer is the one we hear daily from others.

We may hear that we are not worthy. We may hear that we are sinners. We may hear that we are not good enough. We may hear that we are failures. Voices of negativity surround us, and we take those in as our own. Only when we become deliberate about our choice of words can we change our thoughts and our path of action.

Feeding upon negative words prevents us from becoming who we want to be. Our potential for having or becoming is eroded by listening to a story about our lack of worth. Unworthiness is a form of guilt or shame that we carry. We can't have the good outcomes we desire if we don't believe we deserve them.

Using the words "I AM" with positive descriptors dissolves the old reality carried within us by creating an image of who we want to be, while emptying out the stories we've told ourselves for years. It is important to say "I AM" rather than "I want to be," because the word "Want" indicates not having. Would you rather have something or want something?

When you want, something is missing, but when you have, you are complete. This is how "I AM" works. You feel complete, as if you already are the person you desire to be.

You have to be the state before you can own the state. In other words, *you have to make what you desire a part of you as if that desire were real.* The outside is only an illusion of what is inside your mind. You can't own happiness; you can only be happy. You can't own love; you can only be love.

When you hone in on what you desire by becoming the state of your desire, and when you hold that image without contradiction, then you negate your past and exist only in the present. Though we have thoughts from our past, the past does not exist. The past is gone. The present is the only place we can exist. Where we create is in the now.

The only reason we don't get what we want is that we don't think we can. *The problems we have are symptoms of what we think.* Nothing outside of us changes until we change. Using the words "I AM" elicits the change we become.

> *"The closer you come to knowing that you alone create the world of your experience, the more vital it becomes for you to discover just who is doing the creating."*
> — Eric Micha'el Leventhal

NAVIGATE SUCCESS

ALTERING PARADIGMS LEADS TO SUCCESS

Why do people give up? What happens when a dream that seemed so real folds up and disappears from our hearts? We believe we are worthy of our dreams, because we dream them. We might dream about the money we will share to help the homeless, how our words will rise up and be heard by thousands, or how our actions might shape a world of peace. We dreamed as children and believed in our dreams.

And then we grew up and reality hits.

We heard from the naysayers and from those wiser than us, all the things we could not do. And we believed them. We forgot our inner voice, the voice that was there from our beginning, the one daring us to dream, and the one with us as we played and pretended to be what we had not yet become.

We believed until experience proved to us that we could not have our dreams. We blamed reality for our loss, but it wasn't reality. Our loss came from our *perception* of reality.

What is different between those people who reach their goals and those who don't? We want to believe in some mystical fate, so that we can blame the universe. We want to place blame outside of ourselves so we can avoid our own judgment. Then we can say, "I tried, but it wasn't in the cards."

It wasn't in the cards. I didn't get the right hand. Somebody else got all the aces. I got the joker.

We say this when we don't believe that we can have what we desire and don't feel worthy of our dreams. We read obstacles as a sign that we weren't supposed to have what we wanted, and we blame fate. It was not our time, not our destiny, not our providence.

How then do you learn to navigate success?

You change your paradigm. You move from the belief that fate limits your destiny to a belief that you create your own life. When you believe something else pulls your strings and guides you to a limited existence, you limit your power. When your faith guides you, the faith of a greater existence, you behave as if your dream is a bona fide fact.

Switching paradigms requires a shift in your mind. Tony Robbins said, "If you do what you've always done, you will get what you've always gotten."

Wanting to get beyond your failures is not enough: Believe that you SHOULD get beyond them. People who accept failure as a stopping point don't have the faith required to move beyond their obstacles. <u>People who believe in receiving their desires don't view challenges as a stop sign; they see them as green lights to increased opportunities.</u>

Believe that you were born to experience your desires. This is your new philosophy of life.

If you believe that only other people get what they want, then you are not prepared to receive your life in abundance. You are stuck in an old paradigm.

The following people refused to be stuck:

- Steven Spielberg was rejected admission to the University of Southern California twice. He is one of the most prolific filmmakers in history.

- Stephen King's first novel was rejected 30 times. He has now sold over 350 million books.

- Richard Branson has dyslexia. He developed Virgin Airlines and is the fourth richest person in the United Kingdom.

- Oprah Winfrey ran away from home as a young teenager after being repeatedly raped by an uncle, cousin, and a family friend. She now has a net worth of nearly $3 billion.

- Kris Carr overcame a Stage IV cancer called epithelioid hemangioendothelioma. She is now known as one of the most prominent experts in healthy living, with five books and a website followed by over 40,000 people.

As a child I dreamed of being an Olympian. I knew this was my destiny. I felt it. I breathed it. I imagined it daily. It was who I was, not who I was going to become. Then life happened. I was exposed to the jealousy of parents and teammates, and I saw how jealousy can become a cesspool of hatred. After one ninth grade softball game where the spectators in the crowd threatened to take their vocal viciousness to real action, I was escorted off the field by police officers for fear that one of the spectators might harm me. The malicious words of fans and people who I had thought were my friends haunted me. The memory of their malice took on the form of a migraine headache so painful that for two days I couldn't bear light or the tiniest sound.

My challenges with fans and jealousy didn't end there. I was initiated to how people can wield words as swords. This happened during a period in my life before I understood that words cannot wound me without my permission. I accepted those people's malicious actions and words as if they were my truth. In my early paradigm, I was not worthy of other people's love and adoration.

My beliefs affected the way I treated myself and others, which in turn caused more people to treat me poorly. In my senior year of high school, my basketball teammates tried to vote me off the team, and two of my volleyball teammates quit the team rather than play under me as the captain. In college, my teammates wouldn't pass me the ball and refused to sit next to me on the bus.

Did I quit? Yes, a million times in my mind and once physically, but my faith in my dream was bigger than those obstacles.

SUCCESS IS ADVANCED THROUGH STRONG HABITS

When we don't get what we want when we want it, we become frustrated. Why can't we have what we want NOW? The expectation to immediately receive what we want has increased with the onslaught of technological devices that provide things quickly. We don't want to wait more than five minutes for our food, to wade through commercials to watch our television program, or to talk to our friends after work. We want what we want when we want it.

The problem with this mindset is that it doesn't work for all good things. *We can't get what we want if we still are who we were.* We have to transform into a person prepared to receive, and this person needs to form new habits.

Brian Tracy, the top selling author of over 45 books, said, "Successful people are simply those people with successful habits."

If you don't have what you want and you've put some effort into getting your desires, maybe it is time to transform who you are. Most people don't want to hear this, and they certainly don't want to do this. This is why there is a 3% club. Most people are reluctant to change. They want other people to change or life to adapt to them. Those are not viable options, because we have no control over anyone else.

You have to do the work. While this might sound difficult, it is not. The hardest part is getting your mind to accept the need to change and that you are able to change. To do that, you must create new habits. Transforming your habits will make the behaviors consistent that bring you to the life you desire.

You construct a new habit by committing to action every day. Does this sound too overwhelming? At first, the action might be uncomfortable, but you repeat it until it no longer feels uncomfortable.

How long do you need to repeat the action?

Until the habit is developed. This is where people get lost in the process. You have to continue until it works.

Some people believe in a myth that a habit can be created in 21-60 days. Maybe this is true for you, or it could take as few as 18 days or as long as a year to make a new habit. According to research by Lally, van Jaarsveld, Potts, and Wardle (2010) in the *European Journal of Social Psychology,* habits are not formed based on a number of days, but on how motivated the person is to change, and on how problematic and complex the behavior is that needs to be changed.

The important note here is *your* motivation level. If the habit is not changed in 30 days, then you need to persist until the habit is formed. The good news is the more consistent you are in repeating the desired behavior; the faster the desired behavior will become automatic or habitual. If you consistently and persistently repeat the behavior with the intent of creating a new you, and you connect to the positive emotions of the new you, the habit will form faster. **YOU** are the controlling factor.

What habits should you develop? That depends on your goals. If you are an independent sales person, for example, then your new habit might be to reach a certain number of daily contacts. If you are an athlete, you might execute a certain number of daily skills. An author might write a certain number of words per day.

You create the habit that will help you reach your goals. How do you know what habits to set? Ask people who are successful in your field about their habits. If you ask enough successful people, you will discover a system to develop and duplicate.

You do not need to invent a system from scratch. Follow what other successful people have done. They know the secrets, and they didn't create them either. Successful people discovered what the secrets were and created their habits according to those secrets. You don't have to possess special brains or muscles. What you do have to possess is the burning desire to create the necessary habits which have been proven to work.

It is so simple and yet so very complex. By the end of this book, you will have the essential tools to create the changes that you wish. The challenge for you will be to do the compulsory work to change.

FAITH IS A PRECURSOR FOR SUCCESS

Your anxiety has more to do with your lack of faith than your talent.

Faith is the answer to having what you do not yet own but what you understand is yours. Faith is the belief in things unseen yet known to you. When you doubt, you demand to have the experience before you believe in it.

When you cannot believe in something that you have not experienced, you are disconnected between your belief and your desire. You rely on perceptions of your past to determine what is and is not possible. You project your past into the future. As you begin to heal your beliefs you will correct your projections. Then what you do believe, you will actually experience.

This shift to faith is challenging when you believe abundance is scarce and your focus is on what you lack. Your belief in abundance or lack determines your perceptions, which in turn causes you to see what you perceive. The belief in your limitations or lack of abundance causes you to be anxious, worried and frustrated.

Your belief system prevents you from having the very thing that you want, because you are convinced that you lack the possibility. Your mind cannot sustain the faith it needs to persevere when it believes the possibility for having your desires is narrow.

In order to have faith, you must continue. *Faith without perseverance is not faith, but doubt.*

A coaching colleague of mine, Jayson, was firm in his faith. He was one of those men who didn't just talk the talk; he lived it. Jayson's older son suddenly developed what appeared to be a mental illness that took him out of the scope of reality, such that he was hospitalized. The doctors gave Jayson no hope for his son's recovery. Due to his mental illness and his capacity for violence, Jayson's son was heavily drugged.

Despite the doctor's assertion that Jayson's son would not likely recover, Jayson visited his son daily in the hospital. Even though his son was unresponsive, Jayson talked to him, read to him, and told him how much he loved him. He visited his son faithfully for two years.

One doctor asked Jayson, "Why do you continue to come here? Your son can't hear you."

Jayson replied, "Because he is my son and I believe he will be healed."

After two years, Jayson's son was "miraculously" healed. The doctors were dumbfounded.

When I asked Jayson how his son had recovered, he replied, "Faith."

Without faith in something greater, a benevolent source where all goodness and abundance arises, you are disconnected. That disconnection is a barrier between what you want and what you believe you can have. Your fear separates you from your higher self.

Marianne Williamson, author and international lecturer on spiritual, personal, and political issues said, "Love is what we are born with. Fear is what we learn. The spiritual journey is the unlearning of fear and prejudices and the acceptance of love back in our hearts."

When we feel love and are loved, we understand that we are worthy and gravitate toward all of the goodness that exists. We believe there is an abundance of love, and we receive abundant love. That love allows us to experience the beauty of ourselves and our creations.

When you live in fear, you deny yourself all that is good. You teach yourself that you are unworthy of having. You cannot navigate success if you believe you cannot have what is good.

Einstein said, "The single most important decision any of us will ever make is whether or not to believe that the universe is friendly." You get to decide how to perceive the universe. Believing you are separate from love and goodness makes it nearly impossible to gain the mindset that you are worthy of success.

STEPS FOR ACHIEVING THE WIN PHILOSOPHY™

1. What are you willing to do differently than 97% of the

population? List ten ways you will separate yourself from other people so you will be in the top 3%.

2. What are five "I AM" statements that you use daily that impede you from reaching success?

3. Replace those five "I AM" statements with positive statements that will assist you in reaching your desired state of success.

4. What paradigm do you need to change so that you can manifest your dreams?

5. List three habits you are willing to commit to daily which will change your paradigm so you can navigate your success.

CHAPTER TWO

WELCOME YOUR CHALLENGES

LOVING YOUR CHALLENGES

We easily get angry when things don't go our way, when what we want is obstructed from where we are. We believe life is unfair or only the lucky people get their way. We shrink away from our goals when an unforeseen block gets in our path. We might even believe a mystical force robs us of our desires.

This mindset prevents you from success. People aren't just in the right place at the right time or get lucky. Successful people work to be at the right place and position themselves for luck. The successful people prepare, plan and work toward their goals, and when a challenge is presented, they let that challenge stimulate rather than defeat them. They read the challenge as a clue to the next step to motivate them to a higher level, and seize it as an opportunity to grow.

People who have moved from anger to happiness, or poverty to riches, or losing to winning have experienced change as opportunity and have seen potential in crisis. They have used contrast in their lives to gain better insight and know that discomfort accompanies personal growth. When you can shift your anxiety about a challenge to welcoming that challenge, the road to your goals will be much easier. Your dread and apathy will transform into excitement and eagerness.

CHANGE TO RECEIVE

CHANGE IS INEVITABLE

When was the last time you became aware of the need to change, but you feared the actions required to change and the outcome of the change? You might have believed the old platitudes about change:

*Change is hard.

*Change takes time.

*I've been like this all my life. Why change now?

*Change means I'll lose who I am.

*If others don't like me the way I am, it is their problem.

*I might lose my friends if I change.

*You can't teach old dogs new tricks.

*I'm too old to change.

Was your choice to remain stuck rather than face the unknown? Did you ever consider the one constant in life is change? Nothing remains the same except change. Change is inevitable. The clock moves forward. We age. Our bodies alter with time. We move whether we want to move or not. Not only do we change but everything around us is developing. Technology is improving. The phones we use, the cars we drive and the houses we live in are all evolving. Our decision is not whether or not to stop changing; our decision is how we progress.

Everybody changes, but not everybody progresses.

Do you remember being in high school and liking loud music blaring on the car radio? Now, years later, do you turn down the radio the moment your son or daughter cranks it up? When did you begin to prefer listening to the mellow tunes? Did you notice the change before your son cranked up the latest rap song?

Our taste in music often alters without our intention and indicates: 1) We change without conscious effort; and 2) Change can be natural and easy.

If change is a constant, why fight it? Nothing remains exactly the same! You can choose to paddle with the flow of a river or paddle upstream. If you surrender to the idea of constant change, then you are more likely to go with the flow and expand your mental and emotional abilities.

Challenges in your life—physical, mental or emotional—will come. Life gives us opportunities to progress. Some people see and welcome these opportunities, while others fight them and still others give up in defeat. What choice will you make?

FEAR OF CHANGE

Part of what we fear about change is the havoc we think it creates. Change generates the necessity of broadening our comfort zones, stretching us to learn something new and to work harder. When a new policy was introduced at the university, my peers and I moaned and complained about the time it would take. We recognized a learning curve was required and how we would have to rearrange the next few days to learn new procedures. Surprisingly, after moaning and agonizing about it, most of us found our work streamlined and easier. We had *created our discomfort in the fear of our resistance to change.*

Your fear of change distorts the way you view life and derails your determination to move toward new goals. Moving away from the known is uncomfortable. Part of this discomfort is the belief system that remaining where you are is safe and moving forward could produce unnecessary pain. Much of your fear of the unknown lies in the belief system that you have little or no control of your future. When you believe you have the power to create, and that creation of your future is your responsibility, your fears no longer prevent you from tackling new challenges.

Change can be graceful and gradual, and you don't need a lifetime to break through self-defeating patterns which keep you stagnant. Change occurs naturally when you shift from judgment to curiosity, from blame to responsibility, and from fear to faith. The acts of accepting and probing for change assists you in developing the emotional wisdom needed to bypass your fears.

GETTING PAST THE COMFORT ZONE

While you cannot learn all there is to know in a lifetime, at some point you may arrive at a place where you decide you are comfortable without learning anything new. You might have worked in the same job for 22 years, been with your partner for 30 years, or attended the same church for 15 years and settled into the idea that you've attained a level of expertise in those areas. Perhaps so.

But have you reached "emotional expertise?"

Age does __not__ create wisdom. As you age, you accumulate facts and information which do not necessarily transform into wisdom. Wisdom is the intangible quality you gain from experiences as you evaluate and reflect on how those experiences have affected your life. To gain wisdom, you move beyond your "understanding" of your knowledge. You stay open to receive the answers to the *whys* and *hows*, approach questions in a new way, and learn from both your successes and failures.

Many of us are still toddlers when it comes to our emotional wisdom. I've seen prosperous middle-aged men throw temper tantrums at staff meetings, cursing and stomping out of the room when they failed to get their way. I've gone down the same emotional rabbit hole, regressing to three year old tears when criticized in front of peers.

You may be a professor at a university or own a company, but your position does not indicate you have reached emotional wisdom. You've gained wisdom in your chosen profession or you would have lost your job. But how many times has emotional wisdom been forced upon you? Emotional wisdom is a choice. You can choose to bump along with the same awareness you had when you were five, ten or twenty or you can choose to wake up, stop blaming your circumstances or someone else, and take responsibility for creating your desired life.

Emotions can remain at your two-year old irrational self even though your body matures through age and your mind develops through experience. Just because your physical body grows older and changes does not mean your emotional body keeps pace. Emotions remain stuck in the irrational and illogical until you determine to move forward and to train your emotions to go with you.

THE GRANNY SALLY LESSON

My grandmother used to throw her anger at us. She would hurl dishes, yell, use the silent treatment, or any other manipulative behavior she knew to get her way. She had honed these tools since childhood when these behaviors worked with her mother who was too exhausted to deal with her fits and simply gave in to her demands. As my grandmother grew up, she found these same tactics worked with her own family. To avoid confrontation, we waited on her hand and foot. She saw no reason to change her behaviors.

My grandmother created havoc wherever she went, and in response, family members began to avoid her. No one wanted to experience the turmoil she brought with her. As a result, she felt alone and betrayed in her last years. Had she been made more aware that her behaviors were injuring relationships with her loved ones and therefore herself, she might have been more willing to change.

When you tire of the harm stemming from your emotional conditioning—the subconscious beliefs thwarting your happiness, joy, peace, relationships and success—then you have arrived at a place where change does not appear so daunting. Instead change appears necessary. This is the point where you wake up and begin questioning your inner self.

NEW QUESTIONS GET NEW RESULTS

My grandmother had a choice to seethe in anger and self-pity or to become more introspective about the reasons why people stopped coming to visit her. She chose to remain static. Had she chosen progress instead, she could have enjoyed the company of family and friends in her life.

We all choose. <u>We can choose to blame others and stay stuck, or we can to decide to progress and make desired changes in our lives.</u>

Do you want to progress or remain static?

Had my grandmother chosen to progress, her choice would have come from the awareness that she needed new solutions. Instead of asking, "What's wrong with my family?" or "How can they leave me all alone?," she could have asked herself the following questions.

1. Why doesn't my family want to visit me?

2. What have I done to alienate them?

3. If I were to come visit me, would I enjoy the visit? Why or why not?

4. Who is to blame for my behavior? Who is responsible for changing my behavior?

To have family members around her again to celebrate birthdays and holidays, she would have had to recognize she couldn't change us. **BUT,** she could have *changed herself.* This single awareness could have brought love into her life. Because she chose instead to focus on how unloving or unkind her family was, rather than looking at herself, her lonely life did not change.

The **key** here is *to accept that while you cannot change another person, by changing yourself others seems to change.*

Imagine if Granny Sally had picked up the phone and said to me, "I am so sorry I've treated you badly. I can't promise I'll be 100% better, but I will try my best. I'm calling because I miss you, and I want to see you again."

What granddaughter could turn down that request?

The right questions are a powerful catalyst for change. What self-limiting beliefs do you hold? Maybe you've worried, "What if I let everybody down?" Instead ask, "How does it feel when I help my team (family, friends, partner) win?"

Maybe you've asked, "What if I make a mistake?" Try asking, "What would I enjoy learning and who could help me get started?"

Positive questions can unlock the door to new possibilities. Positive questions break through your comfort zone and help you change by choice rather than by chance.

Maybe now is time for you to wake up to change and to reach the success that has eluded you. Change does not have to be difficult, and you do not need another lifetime to break through self-defeating patterns. Change is natural when you shift from judgment to curiosity. You develop emotional wisdom by trying a new approach to life, reflecting on the result, and celebrating when your efforts succeed.

SEE THE OPPORTUNITY IN EVERY CRISIS

THE GLASS IS ALWAYS GOING TO BE EMPTY

You've heard the analogy about the glass. Is it half empty or half full? This simple test will gauge your attitude toward life. Do you see the opportunity in situations or do you see the crisis? Your answer may determine how well you succeed in life.

Growing up, the two most prominent women in my life were my grandmother and mother. They taught me to see the world as half-empty. My grandmother was well schooled in viewing the crisis in every opportunity.

When I was in middle school, I played basketball in our driveway with the boys. When I came in, my grandmother asked me, "Who won the game?"

Proudly I answered, "Me."

"Oh honey, you can't do that. Those boys will never like you. You have to let them win and make them think they are better than you."

Her words destroyed my elation. Instead of celebrating my victories over boys who were bigger, stronger and faster than me, I worried they wouldn't like me.

My mother, living under my Grandmother's roof, also learned how to view the world from the crisis perspective. She saw the worst in every situation and because that is all she saw, she was usually right. As Rumi said, "Whatever you are seeking is seeking you."

In my twenties, I didn't debate with people who theorized about the glass being half-full or half-empty. I viewed the glass as empty no matter what. Either someone else would drink the water, throw it out, or it would evaporate back into the air. The idea that your attitude determined your potential to see the glass as half empty or half full made no sense to me. In the end the glass was empty. Period.

I don't blame my grandmother or mother for their views on life; those views were passed down to them from generations before. Their views were a tradition—one I finally uprooted after 35 years of learning my own life lessons.

A LESSON IN QUANTUM PHYSICS

People listened to my glass theory and called me pessimistic; I replied that my view was realistic.

I thought I saw the world neutrally, without illusion. I believed I saw events, situations and people without coloring the past. What I couldn't take out of the observation was my perspective.

This is where the world of quantum physics comes in to play.

While I do not aspire to fully grasp the science, I understand that one of the main principles of quantum physics is that everything breaks down to energy. When scientists go beyond molecules to atoms and beyond atoms to subatomic particles, they find pure energy. Cars and trees, flowers and bees, you and me, desks, rocks, water, buildings, roads, emotions, air—absolutely everything at its essence is energy.

What is important about this fact? A bit more about quantum physics gets to the point.

Around 1927, a scientist named Neils Bohr got together with other quantum physicists and theorists to explore quantum energy in an experiment that came to be known as the Copenhagen Interpretation.

The experiment tested whether energy existed in the form of waves or particles. Their experiment found something peculiar. The energy under study took the form of the observer. In other words, if a scientist expected to see waves, he saw waves. If another scientist expected to see particles, he saw particles. From this experiment, the scientists concluded that energy was affected by the thoughts and beliefs of the observer.

Everything is made of up energy, including your thoughts, and what you believe creates your experiences.

WOW! What a revelation. So the glass test was real. I saw no possibility of water; therefore, there was none for me. Beyond the empty glass, I saw no possibility of something better, because I was also schooled in Murphy's Law—whatever could go wrong would go wrong at the worst possible moment.

Murphy probably didn't know anything about quantum physics—

if he did, he wouldn't have created the wrong thing happening at the worst moment. Nevertheless I believed in Murphy's Law for years. I was practicing the creation of crisis in my life through my beliefs, and my ignorance did not excuse the results.

How is your glass? Do you expect the best to happen and then find it in your life, or do you seek and find the worst?

WHAT-IF-DOWN THINKING

Imagine for a minute that your work supervisor, Jane, an outstanding professional who you like and admire, is leaving your company to join a major competitor. Your thoughts start spiraling down into a world of negative possibility. They might go like this:

1. Jane has taken a job with our fiercest competitor.
2. She will give them all our trade secrets!
3. Our competitor will have access to our clients.
4. Which means we will lose a fortune.
5. We will have to cut back on our budget.
6. We'll have to lay-off team members.
7. We will lose our most valuable team members to competitors.
8. Eventually we will be forced to close our doors.
9. I will have to file bankruptcy and forget my dreams.

This is what-if-down thinking—the art of creating a nightmare from a neutral story. You start with a small thought and build it up in your imagination until it seems real. How often have you practiced what-if-down thinking in your life?

If observations control your experiences as proved by the Copenhagen Interpretation, then you can change the direction of your life through your thoughts. If you are a what-if-down thinker, you don't have to go down this negative spiral; you can turn your thoughts around. You can change your reality to what-if-up thinking. A what-if-up thinker moves up the scale of possibilities. If you began with the thought Jane was hired by your competitor and saw the positive possibilities which could occur from that event, you would react by searching for constructive outcomes and solutions to the challenge.

Doesn't what-if-up thinking feel better to you? You get excited about what could happen. By simply turning the equation around, you are positively energized. Your eagerness opens you to opportunity. By seeking opportunities, you find them. Whether you are losing a valuable team member or receiving a diagnosis of bad health, what matters is how you think about it.

BELIEVING IN WHAT-IF-UP THINKING

By the time I was 40, my life views were revolutionized. I no longer had to prod myself to be a positive thinker. I felt in charge of my life, and I was teaching my basketball players to think optimistically.

In the world of athletics, winning is crucial— we believe it marks our self-worth. For years I bought into this idea that winning determines worthiness until I realized losing was another opportunity for growth. If we could lose and still find a way to grow, then we hadn't lost at all. I began to understand that the game I was teaching was a vehicle to help others learn the lessons which could make their lives easier.

In 2005, I coached a highly talented team of women. Although the team had incredible athleticism, they were emotionally challenged. It was not unusual for them to fight off the court. They cursed and blamed each other, and fought first with words and later with fists. Every day I put new Band-Aids on gaping emotional wounds in an attempt to keep the team playing together. The next day, the wound would gape wide open once again, and I'd slap another Band-Aid on it.

Yet, this team continued to win. We won so many games that we were ranked in the top ten in the nation and number one in our region. If we won our conference tournament, we hosted the regional tournament giving us a huge advantage to play on our home court. All we had to do was to defeat the teams we had already beaten.

The day before the conference tournament began a fight broke out among some of our key players. My All-American stud, the athlete who took us from average to amazing, called me at 10:30 p.m. She said, "Coach, I refuse to play with this group of morons. I am done with them and their stupidity. Instead of resting over the weekend and preparing for the game, these stupid idiots stayed out late dancing and drinking."

I sat up long past midnight trying to calm down my raging All-American. The next morning instead of preparing for the upcoming game strategizing with our scouting report and walk-through, we stayed in the locker room to dissect the nasty accusations which had flown between teammates the previous night. We were so focused on resolving team issues we didn't have time to focus on tactics for winning the game.

Despite the efforts of my coaching staff and me to resolve the conflict, we couldn't restore team unity. We lost in the semi-finals to a good team, but a team we had beaten earlier in the season. Not only did we lose, we got destroyed with a 20 point blow-out.

By failing to make it to the conference tournament championship game, we lost the opportunity to host the regional tournament.

If I had been in my what-if-down thinking mode, I would have believed this 20 point blow-out meant our chances for winning the regional tournament were over, but I wasn't that person anymore. I was a what-if-up thinker, a person who was searching for the opportunity in every crisis. So, the coaching staff convinced our players losing the ability to host the East Regional Championship was the best thing that could have happened to us.

Here was the what-if-up spiral we fed our team:

1. Playing at another site allowed us an opportunity to spend more time together and to resolve our conflicts.

2. Dining together and hanging out in the hotel would promote better team chemistry.

3. We would feel better about one another.

4. Our positive team chemistry would be a unifying factor.

5. When other teams challenged us, we would be a stronger unit.

6. We would hold together under pressure when other teams folded.

7. All of which foretold we would be walking away with the winning trophy.

The more we talked about how good the loss was for us, the more convinced our players became. The more convinced they became, the more they relaxed. And the more relaxed they became, the better they played.

We had an amazing tournament beating two top ten nationally ranked teams by double digits and becoming the first University of Charleston basketball team to make it to the Elite Eight in the National Collegiate Athletic Association (NCAA) Division II.

If I had been my old self, the what-if-down, empty glass "realist," we would have never won those games. I would have convinced not only myself, but all my players that the conference tournament loss meant losing the dreams of our championship season.

How many times have you experienced this—that when you altered the way you viewed your world that your world changed? A simple shift in thinking can transform the way you view crises. Instead of seeing the crisis in every opportunity, you see the opportunity in every crisis.

George Bernard Shaw said, "Progress is impossible without change, and those who cannot change their minds, cannot change anything."

When you begin to shift your thinking to search for the good in every situation, event or person, you will find it.

The negative is all too easy, because society trains us to see it. We bend events into a soap opera narrative, because it is fun to share bad news and juicy gossip. Many popular magazines and television shows are dedicated to this very concept. Seeking the negative does not enhance your life, however, and it risks bringing into reality that which you seek. Shifting what you seek in life will change what you receive.

How easy is that?

THE CARVE OR STARVE LESSON

How do you move from pessimism to optimism? This process doesn't happen in a minute, an hour or a day. It happens when you decide to change your thoughts. Your decision to choose optimism begins the process.

In the summer of 2001, if you had been walking down the street with me in the quaint little town of Manitou Springs, Colorado, nestled at the base of Pike's Peak hunkered down among pine trees, you would have seen the mountains looming. You would have heard the wind whispering through the aspen leaves and smelled the scent of fresh pine in the air.

If you hadn't been watching closely, you might have walked right past this little wood carver's shop. But if you had stepped inside the store with with me, you would have been enchanted by the lifelike array of animals. Bear, elk, eagles and moose were so lifelike in their cedar carvings, that as I stood transfixed, they appeared to stare right back at me.

A woman approached me, a friendly aging earth mother with deep, thoughtful brown eyes that hinted at years of wisdom and she asked, "How do you like my moose?"

"These are yours? Your carvings are beautiful, and so life-like. How did you learn to carve such amazing pieces?"

She replied, "I was a housewife with two kids when my husband deserted us. I had no job skills and was a high school dropout. All I wanted to do was to be a mother and a wife. I had no means to support myself or my kids. I didn't even know if I could buy enough groceries. One day, desperate for answers, I went outside to walk and calm my mind. I spotted a bit of cedar wood on the ground and picked it up. I remembered as a little girl sitting by my grandfather on the back porch watching him carve wood. One day, he put my hand on top of his hand as he carved out a bear from a piece of cedar. As I remembered that moment on the back porch, it came to me I'd better carve or starve. I've been carving ever since."

This woman's opportunity to be a great artist was disguised in the calamity of her husband's desertion. OPPORTUNITY IS OFTEN DISGUISED AS CALAMITY. Now she shares her art around the world because in the midst of crisis, she uncovered her true potential.

Often we do not see the opportunity in a crisis. Pogo said, "I've seen the enemy and the enemy is me." We might not see our potential. We might not see what good things we can do, for the blindness brought on by believing in all the things we cannot do.

If you were beside me in the locker room on almost any given day during my 23 years of coaching, you would have heard me tell my players the same thing you probably heard from your coaches or parents. Do you remember hearing, "The toughest opponent you will ever face is **YOURSELF**?" Did you believe it? What is stopping you is not the somebody out there, but the somebody inside you.

You are your own biggest adversary. For most people this remains true for their entire lives, because they don't know they can also be their biggest ally.

Do you want to be like most people? Or do you want to be like the artist who found opportunity in her calamity? How will you use the challenges in your life as propulsion to reach your goals? Think about it for a moment. How different are people who ultimately succeed from those who quit? *They both face challenges, but what is different is how they view those challenges.*

I treasure the carve or starve story and the woman who told it to me. I remember her words whenever my life presents a challenge.

I tell myself to choose: "Carve or starve." I remember that an artist created beauty at a time in her life when she was frightened, lonely and desperate. Her tenacity taught me that in the midst of crisis, I too have an opportunity to create and bring beauty to life.

CONTRAST POINTS
THE WAY TO YOUR DESIRES

AWARENESS IS YOUR ROAD MAP

When was the last time you got frustrated, anxious, or worried when you didn't get what you desired? Perhaps you dreamed as a teenager of being a top executive in a large corporation, but when you achieved that goal, you found it unsatisfying. You didn't feel the freedom that you imagined. The long hours and great salary didn't make up for the time spent away from family, vacations, and doing the things you loved. This contrast between what you thought you wanted and the resulting experience made you feel uncomfortable. This contrast provided an impetus for you to search for other opportunities.

Contrast is your road map to awareness.

AND Awareness is the first step to getting what you desire.

Many times when we are in the throes of contrast, we don't feel good. We don't like what we are experiencing, and we can't see how that experience will help us reach our desires. What we don't understand is we view life through a periscope. We see a sample of what is in our world, and we can't see what is outside our view. We don't possess the broader vision to know if our current experience will help us get what we want in life.

Then we lose faith. We get discouraged and aggravated with our lives. The truth in this lesson is that we are learning what we don't want. It is only through this contrast that we learn what we do want.

Life is a buffet. As you go through the line, you pick up all sorts of events that appeal to you. Once you taste them, though, you may learn that you didn't like the experience that you chose. So you go back and get in the buffet line again, but this time you are more selective. Because you understand your tastes better, you pick and choose with more care. The more you know about what you desire, the more successful you are at selecting better opportunities. As your desires constantly evolve, you continue to select from this buffet of life. You progress through the experiences of tasting different life events.

UNDERSTANDING THE PROCESS

In 1981 I began three years of grueling training for the 1984 Olympic Games to compete in team handball, a sport similar to soccer using the hands or water polo on land. From 1981 until 1984, my team trained twice a day all year long.

If you don't know what training that hard feels like, pretend it snowed and you spent an hour shoveling your sidewalk. Imagine shoveling that snow six hours a day. Now imagine shoveling that snow for six hours every day for three years.

With that image in mind, think about how you would feel shoveling the same sidewalk every day in the morning and again in the evening. That is how I felt when training with the national team handball team. We did the same skill workout every morning, day after day, and then we scrimmaged with the same teammates every evening.

Why the monotony, you might ask? You would have had to ask our Czechoslovakian coach, Klement Capliar. Personally,

I thought the repetition stemmed from Klement being lazy and only knowing a few English words: "Two groups, two teams, two hours, two times, two halves. Let's go!"

Worse than the monotonous training sessions were his standardized pregame speeches. Before every game we played, Klement gave us the same pregame speech, "Are you ready, are you really, really ready? To run fast, fast, fast as you can? To play as hard, hard, hard as you can? Now, let's go win. Win two halves."

Can you imagine how that speech left my team uninspired?

I will always remember the day the monotony of his pregame speech finally broke. Klement was droning on to my teammates with his infamous, well-worn pre-game speech. Cindy Stinger, the team star, was putting new shoelaces in her high-top, white and blue Puma shoes. I looked around the locker room and noticed that 14 pair of eyes were riveted on Cindy lacing up her shoes. Not only did we want contrast; we craved contrast.

Coach Klement couldn't bring a pregame speech that was more interesting than watching Cindy lace up her shoes. That scene stayed in my mind because he showed me the kind of coach I did NOT want to be—a coach without passion or imagination. His failure filled me with ideas on how to motivate and inspire my own teams.

The first time I sat on the bench as a three-year-old watching my mother coach her junior high basketball team, I knew I wanted to be a coach. From that moment forward, I experienced the contrast of various coaching styles. Klement's coaching style proved to me what type of coach I did not want to become. Lessons learned firsthand are powerful teaching aids. When you learn what you don't want, you are really <u>learning what you do want. This contrast points you toward your desires.</u>

Think of an event right now from your past that you did not appreciate at the time. Can you see how that event gave you the contrast you needed to push you a new direction?

LEARNING TO VALUE THE PROCESS

Most of us do not appreciate contrast showing up in our lives, because we don't grasp how contrast points toward success. My contrast experience was provided by a poor Olympic coach. He gifted me the wisdom to become a great coach.

We forget that the very thing we fight not to experience may propel us forward, expand us and move us in a new direction. You would not be who you are today without experiencing contrast. The trick is to appreciate the contrast while you are in the moment. Why do this? *Because appreciation lets you experience even the difficult moments with clarity and energizes you toward what is good in your life.*

How does contrast energize you?

Contrast teaches you to appreciate your experiences when people:

- Abandoned you, for they taught you self-reliance.
- Betrayed you, for they taught you loyalty.
- Rejected you, for they taught you acceptance.
- Hated you, for they taught you love.
- Gave you grief, for they taught you joy.
- Judged you unworthy, for they taught you to see value in others.

Having faith that contrast in your life pushes you toward your desires changes your attitude. You see events differently. You understand that your life journey is a process, and you don't get bogged down in the moment.

What is another way you can practice getting through the moment? An attitude of gratitude.

An attitude of gratitude raises your energy by acknowledging all the people, events and things for which you are thankful. Think of yourself as going on a rampage of appreciation.

Who do you say thank you to? To your higher power. To yourself. To your family. To your teammates, your co-workers and your friends. To anyone and everyone.

Thank you for my family. Thank you for my friends. Thank you for my dogs. Thank you for all the times I have traveled safely. Thank you for Coach Klement, who taught me the wrong way to coach so that I could discover the right way to coach. Thank you. Thank you. Thank you.

When I practice an attitude of gratitude, I improve my outlook on life, and I'm sure you will too. Look for the good things that occur in your life. Practice turning your mind toward what is good, and you will discover that by doing this, you anticipate the future and reach better outcomes.

SEEING THE GOOD IN THE CONTRAST CHANGES THE OUTCOME

I was coaching at the University of Charleston in October of 2009. I held a short informational meeting with my team members before practice. I provided life lessons to my players, because I knew that being a good player wasn't enough. They needed to grow in character. This growth aided them on and off the court, giving them the ability to excel. On this particular day, I shared the value of including an attitude of gratitude in their daily rituals.

After my gratitude spiel, we headed to the court for practice. About five minutes into practice, I was not appreciative of their efforts. They were lazy, failing to give 100% effort into our drills.

Have you ever been around somebody who was goofing off when you were trying to lead a group? Do you remember how frustrating that was? I had one player, Jihan, who knew how to hit all my buttons. She constantly told jokes on the sideline and goofed off when I was coaching.

I drove four and a half hours to Cleveland High School Jihan's senior year to watch her play. When I arrived, she wasn't in the gym. It was 20 minutes before game time and both teams were going through pregame warm-ups. With 17 minutes left on the pregame clock, Jihan sauntered, not rushed, but sauntered into the gym, stopping to chat with several fans in the stands. She grabbed some potato chips from a fan, went to her team bench, sat down, and ate chips while her teammates continued warming up on the floor.

You are probably wondering right now why in the world I recruited her. Trust me, I asked the same question to myself every single day for three years.

On this particular day, I was coaching from my position just inside half court while Jihan was on the baseline talking to a teammate. I blew my whistle, gave Jihan my death stare and said, "Jihan, why don't you just share with the whole team what you think is so important THAT YOU CAN TALK WHILE I'M COACHING?"

Jihan nonchalantly stepped onto the court, put her hands on her hips and said, "I am thankful I have such a great coach. I am thankful that you are a patient and kind. AND I am so thankful that you think I am funny."

It turned out that humor did have a place on the team. Once I came to appreciate the contrast that Jihan brought to the team, I was able to coach her more effectively. We stopped butting heads. Working together, we achieved a 26-7 record, and Jihan, the smart-alecky girl who had sauntered onto a high school basketball court and stopped to eat chips and chat with her fans, made remarkable improvements. For three seasons she never was good enough to be voted an All-Conference Player, but that year she averaged double digits in both rebounds and points. She became our go-to player, and was voted first team All-Conference and an All-American.

DISCOMFORT NUDGES YOU TO GROW

Do you remember a challenge that you believed was the worst that ever happened to you, and it turned out to the best thing that ever happened to you? Can you remember how that journey impacted you?

In 1996, after having tremendous success at Montana State University Northern where I had a record of 139 wins versus 20 losses, five conference championships, and a national title, I made the transition to the University of Southern Colorado where the program had a losing tradition. I departed Northern thinking I wanted more challenges. That thought soon evaporated.

I resided in Pueblo for four weeks when the pain hit. It wasn't an agonizing pain, at least not at first. The pain started in my right lower back, crept down my thigh into my calf and finally into my toes. I reacted like most athletes; I kept pushing through the pain. Only this pain didn't subside. In fact, it kept getting worse.

The pain became so intense that I didn't want to sit, stand or walk. Did that stop me? Not initially. I was a two-time Olympian. I was tough. I had played through bumps and bruises, strained ligaments and muscles, sprained ankles, and a broken finger, nose and toe. None of those things stopped me from playing for long. In fact, during my entire career I never sat out longer than a couple of games.

BUT this pain…this pain was more than I could handle. The pain became so intense that I quit working out and became a couch potato. Not only could I no longer do the things I loved to do, I couldn't push a grocery cart through a store long enough to buy groceries. I couldn't even go to a movie at the theatre, because I couldn't stomach sitting that long.

I thought I'd go to the doctor, take a few pills, have a little surgery, rest and be done with it. The first doctor who examined me told me I was suffering from some of the symptoms of getting old. I WAS 33! That was the same year that John Elway quarterbacked the Denver Broncos to the Super Bowl. He was 34.

For the next two years, I scheduled appointments with specialists. I saw neurologists, back specialists, orthopedists, chiropractors, physical therapists, and massage therapists. I had every test known to mankind: MRI's, ultrasounds, blood tests, x-rays, cat scans, and bone scans. I even went to a psychic. Nobody had any answers.

My pain got worse. All the doctors knew how to do was to prescribe pain medications and I refused to take them. I didn't want to mask the pain; I wanted to discover the cause of the pain.

What most people don't know about chronic pain is how it affects the mind. People with chronic pain get depressed. They become hopeless. They become suicidal. I was all of those.

After two years of empty answers, I went to my last doctor. He took all my tests and told me he was going to get a group of renowned specialists together. They would review my charts and come up with a game plan for me. For the first time in two years, I got excited. I would have a game plan, keys to becoming healthy again. I'd be able to run, hike, backpack and bike. I'd be me again.

When I went back to the doctor he said, "After reviewing your files, we've come up with a solution. We think you should go to a pain management clinic."

"What happened to the game plan?"

"That is the game plan."

I got up off the examination table and walked to the door. "I don't like your game plan. It doesn't sound like a winner to me. You don't get me, do you? I don't want to manage the pain; I want to get rid of it."

He walked toward me. "Listen. You are making a mistake. There are no answers for this type of pain. The only way to get better is to learn how to manage the pain."

I left without saying another word. I refused to accept the diagnosis of the 17 medical professionals I had seen.

The journey to health was a long one. It didn't come easy. I researched. I studied. I searched for alternative answers. I tried the Egoscue Method which was a series of exercises strengthening supportive muscles. Pete Egoscue, the founder of the Egoscue

Method, theorized muscles moved the bones and held them in place. By strengthening the muscles, my bones would shift and remain in place preventing pain from occurring. I had some success with this program. In fact, I was able to resume a somewhat normal life by doing the 90 minutes of special Egoscue Exercises every morning. I did this for five years. The problem was that I wasn't improving; I was surviving. I'd do the exercises in the morning which allowed me to function throughout the day and then by the evening I was back in pain.

I decided to take another step toward my health. I tried Integrative Manual Therapy (IMT), a therapy which works on the body, mind and spirit. The first time I tried it, I thought it was a bunch of rubbish. Those therapists told me that my pain wasn't all physical. It was related to my thoughts and emotions. I got off the table and left those imposters behind in their office. I knew that wasn't emotion in my leg; that was bona fide physical pain.

How desperate do you have to be before you open your mind to new possibilities? I wasn't desperate enough yet to open my mind. It took another two years of pain before I decided to try IMT again.

It took me another five years to get healthy enough to play like I wanted to play. It probably wouldn't have taken so long if I wasn't so stubborn. I didn't want to work on my emotions. I couldn't see the link between thoughts and health. I could link thoughts to attitude and attitude to feeling better, but I refused to imagine that thoughts could affect my health.

The result of my journey to a healthier body was a total makeover of mind, body and spirit.

It was my chronic pain that pushed me forward and it was chronic pain which nudged me to see life differently. Behind the words in this book are the lessons I've learned from the discomfort which caused me to grow.

What type of lessons have you learned from the adversities in your life?

Everybody experiences challenges. They are different for each of us and they nudge us to become somebody different. Maybe your challenges taught you to be authentic, to be humble, and to love yourself more. Perhaps your challenges taught you the power of forgiving others and yourself. Love your challenges because they open you up to greater possibilities and to see things that you never dreamed of.

Brock Phillips said it in a way that I wished I had:

> *"Do not pray for easier lives ... pray to be stronger people. Do not pray for tasks equal to your powers ... pay for powers equal to your tasks. Then the doing of your work shall be no miracle, but you shall be a miracle."*

You are a miracle. We are all miracles. Sometimes we need to be nudged to remember the miracle we are.

FIVE STEPS TOWARD SEEING THE OPPORTUNITIES

1. Look at your past. Write down three events which you initially labeled as bad. Beneath each one of them, write five constructive things that occurred as the result of this event.

2. When an event occurs in your life that feels bad to you, write down ten positive possibilities which could evolve from this event. Keep an open mind here. Be creative

and free flowing.

3. Take one thought that you have spiraled into what-if-down thinking. Turn it around to write what-if-up thoughts. Make certain to complete at least seven what-if-up thoughts.

4. Play the what-if-possibility game every day for a month. This will take 2-3 minutes. Give yourself as many what-if constructive dream thoughts as you can without allowing yourself to answer. It becomes one long stream-like continuous question of possibilities.

   For Example:

   What if I could travel anywhere in the world I wanted? What if I could get on a plane to Spain tomorrow? What if I could go on a Safari in Africa? What if I could boat the Amazon? What if I could visit the ruins of Greece? What if I could travel first class? What if I could stay in the presidential suites of the best hotels? What if... what if...what if....

   This practice allows you to see possibilities and to feel them. When you don't allow your mind time to answer, you actually feel as if those things could happen. This practice raises your vibration.

5. Place a half full glass of water on the table. Take a bowl of water and a tablespoon. Think of a positive thing you can focus on today. Take a tablespoon of water from the bowl and pour it into in the glass. Continue doing this until your glass is full. Whenever you look at that glass of water, think about how easy it was to fill it full of possibilities. That glass is forever full as long as you continue to fill it.

CHAPTER THREE

IMPROVE YOUR COMMUNICATION SKILLS

COMMUNICATION
IS THE RELATIONSHIP

EVERYTHING IS A CONVERSATION

Everything in your life is fundamentally a conversation. Conversations are how you communicate with yourself, your loved ones and your peers. Most of the conversations are ones you have with yourself, and sometimes you allow other people to become part of your conversation. The internal words you use through your thoughts and interpersonal conversations are potent. It is why the first step to becoming a true winner is listening to your words.

We have between 40,000 and 60,000 thoughts per day. How many conversations are in our thoughts? How many of those conversations are rooted in the past obsessed with our mistakes, combating our guilt and shame? These conversations are based on events that we cannot change, yet we ceaselessly worry about them. Instead of focusing on the now, we think about things which are irreversible. The problem we encounter with these conversations about our past is that most of them hinge on the same conversations we have had with ourselves thousands of times.

In fact, we think the same thoughts 98% of the time. Reiterating the same thoughts would be wonderful if those thoughts were positive. Unfortunately about 70-80% of our thoughts tend to hover around negative substance.

THE OPTIMIST TEST

You might think, as I did, that you are a positive thinker. You tell other people you are an optimist. I'd like to challenge you to do an experiment that my friend, Maggie, challenged me to do.

Maggie Cook, the creator and owner of Maggie's Salsa, believes everything begins and ends with the mind. By changing her mind about her past, she created a million dollar business by the time she was 33.

Maggie was born in Mexico, a natural born daughter of two missionaries who adopted over 50 children. Even though she was the birth child of her parents, she was treated the same as all the adopted children. She slept in the barracks, washed her clothes on a scrub board, and bathed in the creek. Many times in her childhood, she did not know where the next meal was coming from, and she was often sent into the woods to hunt for game to be used as food.

Maggie possessed several reasons to succumb to failure. She had a history and a thought pattern to explain her poverty, but instead she chose to change her thinking. She created her business through the process of reading and listening to personal development books.

In May of 2013, Maggie challenged me to listen to my thoughts for three consecutive days, and to rewire my negative thoughts by saying, "I choose to release this thought and replace it with love." Since I was a person who had worked on my thoughts for years, my belief was that this would be an easy challenge for me.

Within an hour, I discovered how many negative things I continually told myself.

- "My shoulder hurts."
- "I'm tired."
- "I didn't get enough sleep last night."
- "I'm getting old."
- "I wish my hair didn't have that cowlick."
- "I hate that my teeth are crooked."
- "I don't know if I'm smart enough to make it in this business."
- "I should have stayed in coaching."

WOW! I spent the first hour releasing negative conversations and realizing how much I still needed to change.

How many negative conversations have eluded your awareness?

THE WORDS YOU ARE SPEAKING ARE SPEAKING YOU

Neale Donald Walsch in *Conversations With God: An Uncommon Dialogue, Volume 1*, said, "What's happening is merely what's happening. How you feel about it is another matter."

Have you had a repeated conversation about your weaknesses? Perhaps you said, "I'm not smart enough to create my own business." If you've had that conversation, chances are you sought more evidence to support your theory. The more you seek something, the more evidence you will find. You connect patterns in your brain through seeking evidence to support your theories.

The more you loop the same thoughts over and over again, the more those same thoughts will be connected. Your thoughts actually start thinking you, rather than you thinking your thoughts. The more evidence you seek and the more you believe in your evidence, the more you will experience the truth you created. You are not thinking original thoughts but repeating old ones, which in turn drive your actions.

Neale Donald Walsh also said, "Belief creates behaviors."

When you allow your conversations "to create you" without intervention, you are a spectator in your own life. When I was nineteen, I thought life happened to me so when my teammates at Texas A&M felt I was not a good fit with the team, I told myself what I had been telling myself for years, "Nobody likes me." This was a story that began when my mother sang the "Worm Song" to me as a baby and a toddler. I then sang the song to myself as a youngster believing the lyrics were true:

Nobody likes me. Everybody hates me. I'm going to eat some worms. First you get the bucket, then you get the shovel. Oh, how they wiggle and squirm.

Since I didn't know I could change my dialogue, I continued repeating the same thoughts. I told myself "Nobody liked me" and expected positive results through my negative words. It was ironic how other people picked up on my negative thoughts, and then assisted me in perpetuating experiences where I was the outcast. Unknowingly I created events believing the entire time I was not a participant in my life but a spectator of my life.

Negative phrases and complaints are exhausting. They drain your dreams and diminish what you believe is possible. They demoralize your belief in self and cause corresponding chemicals to be released in your body which actually weaken your physiology. These negative thoughts cause you to be more fatigued.

You have the power to change your inner dialogue just like I did. Instead of saying, "Nobody likes me," I chose to say, "I am liked by everybody, because I am kind and compassionate." This change in thinking created a corresponding alteration in the chemicals released by my body, which boosted my energy.

When you alter your thoughts to more positive destinations, not only are your thoughts no longer thinking you; they are no longer determining how you feel. You generate a better environment inside of you which gives you the power to generate a better environment outside of you.

THE FOUR C'S OF COMMUNICATION:

Once you understand the major conversation is with yourself and how you talk to yourself determines how you communicate with others, then you are prepared to take the next step toward better conversations with other people.

These four steps are:

1. Be **conscious** if what you say is what you meant to say.

2. Take the time to **comprehend** what others are saying.

3. Allow people to **challenge** what you have said.

4. **Create** the relationship you desire through effective communication.

BE CONSCIOUS

How many times have you thought you clearly and concisely conveyed your message only to discover what other people heard was gibberish? Did you blame them for their inability to hear, or get angry when they failed to follow your requests? Or did you question how clearly you communicated your message?

Imagine you are a woman and come home one night determined to have an honest conversation with your husband. You say, "I need to talk to you. I am so exhausted. We both work full time jobs, and when I come home I'm too tired to do all the work. I need some help."

Your husband puts his arm around you, kisses you on the forehead and says, "I hear you. I'm so glad we had this talk. I love you."

The next day you come home expecting the dishes to be in the dishwasher, the floor to be vacuumed and the clothes to be folded from the dryer. What you find is a dozen red roses on the table with a note which says:

I hope you feel better today. I love you. P.S. I'll be home late for dinner. I'm playing golf with the guys.

You react in anger. Why didn't he listen to you? It appears you wasted all that time overcoming your fears to converse about the unfairness of the household responsibilities. You were initially relieved when you thought he heard you, but now it appears that he either brushed you off or failed to hear your pleas. After you cooled off and examined the conversation in depth, you realized you failed to convey your needs. What you said didn't line up with what you meant. Your husband interpreted your words to mean that you needed emotional support, which he provided.

Most of the struggles we have with our spouses, partners, friends, and team members come from our inability to communicate effectively. Since we cannot control the other person in the communication process, it is up to ourselves to be aware of the techniques we use.

When you are conscious of how you communicate, you realize how easy it is to misinterpret conversations. You clarify your intentions by clearly defining what you want in a way that is constructive.

An easy way to be constructive is to state your **concern**. "When I get home from work, I'm exhausted. I'm **concerned** how this exhaustion is affecting our relationship."Notice the use of "I" statements and how there is no accusation or blame in the sentence. The sentence is meant to get the attention of your spouse without creating the need for defensiveness.

Use the next statement to make a **constructive request**. Requests are less likely to create division and more likely to signal the willingness to work together on a solution. "Honey, would you agree to split the household chores with me? Can we discuss what portion of those chores you would be willing to take?" You engage your spouse in the conversation giving him the opportunity to respond while still directing the conversation.

While creating this conscious conversation, ask yourself: "Am I clearly conveying what I want? Is there an easy way to misinterpret my desires?"

Before departing the conversation, make certain the issue is resolved. Ask: 1) Are we evading any topic which needs to be addressed? 2) What is our mutual agreement? 3) Have we discussed the root of the issue? 4) Is there anything we haven't discussed which we need to discuss?

Conscious communication takes effort, and the rewards of improved relationships are worth the effort.

HAVE THE INTENTION TO COMPREHEND

What is the opposite of speaking? Most people answer, "Listening," but is that the truth? What most people do during a conversation is wait to talk. They form responses, advice, judgment, and stories they want to share.

In 2012, I sold my log house in West Virginia and was preparing to move to Montana when I came home to a note hung on my doorknob. The property tax evaluators had requested me to contact them. When I called the conversation went something like this:

> ME: "Hi. I'm Sherry Winn and I received a message tacked to my door. I wanted to clarify some issues with you so that you can talk to the new owners of the house. I recently sold my house but I noticed you had the wrong address on the card."
>
> MAN: "Okay."
>
> ME: "Who am I speaking to?"
>
> MAN: "Joe."
>
> ME: "Joe, the address has been changed to the house. It is the same house in the exact same location but it is no longer 2041 Martins Branch Dr. It is now 225 Cheyenne Lane. That is 225 Cheyenne Lane."
>
> JOE: "So how did you move the house? Is it trailer house or a modular? Did you put it on one of them big trucks?"

ME: "No, I didn't move the house. The address has been changed due to the new 911 codes so the fire department can locate the house."

JOE: "You had a fire at the house? Man, that guy who bought it from you must be a sucker."

ME: "No Joe. There was no fire. The address was changed so emergency vehicles could properly locate the house."

JOE: "What was the emergency? Was somebody hurt during the fire?"

ME: "No, there was no fire. The address was changed for emergency crews."

JOE: "So was the emergency a flood?"

ME: "No. Look, Joe I'm just going to give you the name and the phone number of the new owner."

JOE: "Wait. Wait. Wait. Let me find a pen and paper so I can write this down and give it to the guy who does this sort of thing."

I laughed as I hung up the telephone. Joe was in desperate need of a workshop on active listening. He was a prime example of what happens when a person is waiting to talk rather than listening.

The problem with being an active listener is that you have to forget about YOU for a while. That is why listening is so hard. Most of us don't listen or try to comprehend what somebody else is saying, because we are too busy thinking about what we want to say. Great communicators spend their time listening and then determining how they can ask another question which clarifies the subject matter, digs deeper into the person's story, or helps the other person come to a new self-awareness.

Joe could have shown his ability to comprehend my statements by actively questioning me. He could have said, "When you said you changed your address, did you mean that you changed locations?" When I responded "NO" we are on an entirely different conversation.

Joe could have said, "What I heard you say was that you sold your fire-damaged house to a sucker. Is that correct?" No Joe.

Or he could have been like most people who are having their own conversations in their heads, and kept asking questions about the fire that never happened.

In order to comprehend others better, be present when they are speaking. When they stop speaking, let silence linger for five to ten seconds so they have an opportunity to finish their thoughts. Clarify what you thought you heard by restating what they said or asking questions. While you cannot determine how somebody else communicates, you do have the ability to determine your comprehension.

BE OPEN TO CHALLENGES

What prevents most people from stating their true feelings is the fear of the other person's reactions. Most people are not receptive to challenges and react illogically, irrationally, defensively, or even aggressively. Are you somebody who allows other people to challenge you?

When I was a collegiate basketball coach, I thought I was a great communicator. I allowed my players, who were decades younger than me, to have a voice on the basketball court. I asked them what they thought and valued their opinions. I often inquired, "Does anybody have any questions?" Because my players rarely answered this question during timeouts, games, or at halftimes,

I assumed my communication was clear.

Let's put this assumption into play.

It is halftime. The University of Charleston Golden Eagles are down by 5 points. I come in the locker room, passionate about the outcome of the game. My shirt sleeves are rolled up, the back of my shirt is halfway out of my pants, and my suit jacket is off, having been tossed behind the bench when the opponents stole the ball and went down for a lay-up. My hair is wayward from the numerous times I've put my hands on top of my head in total disbelief of what is occurring on the court. Sweat is rolling down my forehead, and my eyes are wider than half dollar bills. The vein in my throat snakes it way into my shirt collar. Froth is coming out of my mouth.

"LADIES, I KNOW YOU KNOW HOW TO DEFEND THEIR ELEVATOR PLAY. WE'VE GONE OVER IT A HUNDRED TIMES IN PRACTICE. IT IS ESSENTIAL THAT WE STOP THEM FROM SCORING ON IT."

I go to the whiteboard, draw a diagram of the court. As I diagram the play, I never wipe off the board. I simply keep marking lines, numbers and letters all over the place. The entire time I'm in full coaching mode—excited, focused and gesticulating wildly.

The diagram behind me looks like a frog smashed by a bulldozer. I point at it. "Is this clear? Does anybody have any questions?"

When the players answer me with silence, I say, "ALL RIGHT THEN. YOU KNOW WHAT TO DO. LET'S GET IT DONE. I DON'T WANT TO SEE THEM SCORE OFF THAT PLAY AGAIN." As we walk back onto the court, I am pleased with myself. I am a great communicator. Every single one of my players understood what they needed to do, because nobody questioned me.

This, of course, is an illusion. What player in her right mind would question a coach who looks like a coke addict needing a fix?

The next day I enter the locker room where the players are having a contest to see who can define what the diagram on the white board most resembles. Their answers:

- A cow having a calf under water.

- A missile imploding on a pan of lasagna.

- Three half-digested donuts in a stomach.

- An infected intestine.

- A three year olds rendition of a dinosaur.

That was the moment I decided to question how effective my communication efforts were. If my players couldn't understand the drawing on the whiteboard, what other pieces of my communication did they not understand? How was I preventing myself from receiving important knowledge if I projected an image which clearly said, "Don't ask unless you are prepared for the coming onslaught of crazy emotions."

Have you had an "Ah-ha!" moment where you discovered that you didn't allow other people to challenge you? Are you missing vital information, because your team or family members are afraid to honestly communicate with you?

Some insecure people may never feel comfortable having honest conversations. You may never get feedback from them, but there are other people around you who would be willing to offer valuable information if they thought you would be receptive. What you don't know because you protect your ego from challenges doesn't hurt them, it hurts you.

CREATE THE RELATIONSHIP YOU DESIRE

You establish positive relationships by becoming conscious of your statements, comprehending other people, and allowing people to challenge your words. When you communicate in this manner, you value others. People who feel valued are more likely to work harder and remain in the same position longer.

A key gauge of job performance is feeling valued. Team members who feel valued are more likely to show contentment and fulfillment in their jobs, which transpires to higher levels of engagement. A majority of the American work force list work as a significant source of stress, which lowers their work productivity. Almost half of those workers who reported high levels of stress also indicated they didn't feel valued at their jobs. Most people join companies but leave due to poor managers.

To keep your team members happy and productive, form an environment where communication is encouraged, integrity is valued, and workers feel their voice is heard.

It doesn't matter where you practice you communication skills--at home, in the office, or on a golf course with friends. What does matter is how your words and listening skills impact those around you. Other people return their trust and loyalty when they believe in your integrity and compassion.

PROVIDING FEEDBACK

THE BUY-IN: CRITICISM IS NOT PERSONAL

We depend upon our strengths to reach our potential. We suffer in our deficiencies when we allow them to interfere with our abilities. Individuals who value and accept coaching from others address their weaknesses quicker, because they listen and make the necessary adjustments.

One of the most critical factors in accepting coaching is to comprehend that constructive feedback is not personal. It is a necessary component of building talents. Constructive feedback is an offering from individuals who care enough to illustrate a superior method or present a shortcut to success.

We can present constructive feedback in numerous ways; and no matter how selective we are in choosing our methods, we should be aware the receiver of our feedback is being informed her effort is not up to standard. *This means that no matter how carefully you phrase your feedback, it might not be heard as you intended.* I learned that my players often did not hear the positive feedback we gave them.

My players never touched a basketball, lifted weights, or ran a wind sprint before we talked about the importance of being coached, which was defined as the ability to accept feedback from both coaches and teammates. Throughout the season we continued to stress that our constructive feedback was essential toward improving each individual and creating a championship team.

Our coaching staff spoke positive language, giving as many warm, fuzzy statements as we could when we were coaching. Our intention was to build our players up through our feedback, never speaking words which demeaned or demoralized them. We focused on channeling our energy toward helping them improve their behaviors and skills.

Despite our conscious efforts to build our players' confidence, we discovered a majority of our players left practice thinking they had done nothing right. This was the result of typical reactions to constructive feedback. Our players, like most people, were too focused on hearing the negative rather than emphasizing the positive.

In order to help our players hear our compliments, we instituted a rule from Pat Summit, the famous head basketball coach of the University of Tennessee who won over 900 games in her career. Under the Summit Rule, we required our players to say, "Two points" every time they heard positive feedback. When they heard constructive criticism, they responded with "Rebound." The idea was that they would hear themselves saying "Two points" much more frequently than "Rebound."

The Summit Method ensured our players heard positive feedback. It gave the coaches a reference to how many times we used positive statements versus constructive feedback.

Maybe this idea sounds too juvenile for your company, family or yourself, but it works. You might want to choose different language or a different reward system, but the most important thing is to find a way to effectively communicate constructive and positive feedback.

HOW THE WORD "BUT" CAN RUIN ANY FEEDBACK

Being positive helps those around you hear your feedback, and there are times when you have to coach your people to higher levels of competency. You don't receive optimal results when you allow people to be less than their capabilities.

One of the words which can destroy all your intentions to provide instructive coaching tips is the word, "But." The word "But" is a contrary conjunction. It is contrary, because it defies all the words that precede it. No matter what optimistic words you provide, you kill them all when you connect your compliment to your coaching tip with *but.*

You do the same to yourself when you pronounce, "I am smart, *but* I struggle with doing math problems." You are providing yourself with two multiple realities. Both of the statements are true, and it is up to you to decide which one of them you believe. The problem with this approach is that we tend to believe the negative statement, because we have been taught to see ourselves as less than we are. We are taught to downplay our strengths and focus on our weaknesses. After all, who loves the cocky and the arrogant?

When you provide coaching tips to others and use the word, "But," your statement has two possible realities. You give them an option to believe your first statement or your second statement. When you tell your team member, "You have the uncanny ability to see the solutions inside our challenges, **but** you don't know how to get your team members on board with you to coordinate the solution," you place the two realities in direct competition with one another. You supply an underlying truth which stands out stronger than the compliment. In this situation, you provide a win-lose scenario. You win and your team member loses.

When you substitute the word "And" in your coaching tips, you offer a cooperative conjunction. You can have two separate and true realities.

"I am smart, *and* I struggle doing math problems."

"You have the uncanny ability to see the solutions inside the challenges, *and* you don't know how to get your team members on board with you to coordinate the solution."

The two statements are not competing against one another, so they can both exist and can both be true. Exchanging one three letter word for another one doesn't seem like a big deal, **and** it can be the deal breaker between the willingness and the resistance to being coached.

THE KEYS TO GENUINE CONVERSATIONS

PREVENT YOUR EGO FROM TAKING CENTER STAGE

How many times have you had a conversation with somebody who was sad, anxious, worried, or nervous, and when they left, you felt great about the advice you gave them? Did you offer stories about yourself, the ways you overcame your challenges, and give them a remedy for their situation?

Answer this question honestly. Was the conversation more about you or about the person you were helping? Did your ego get in the way of the conversation? If you did more talking than questioning and listening, then you made the conversation about you.

I've had those conversations. As a basketball coach, I was older than my players; therefore, my belief was I had more substance, insight and wisdom. They needed to know what I knew. I had suffered through chronic pain, the humiliation of being fired, and the darkness of depression. I possessed the juju, the magic formula to cure all ailments. While my players spoke, I mixed enchanted formulas in my head ready to disperse them the moment they stopped for a breath.

I couldn't wait to fix them and then to congratulate myself for a job well done. The problem with this tactic was that when my players didn't come to awareness on their own terms, they didn't hear it as well. They left without the impetus needed to move forward, because it wasn't their Ah-ha moment. It was medicine for my ailment. I projected my past onto them, offering advice based on my autobiography.

One of the challenges of listening is to *really* listen and to keep the conversation about the other person. How do you do this? You ask reflective questions. A reflective question frames what the speaker said without additional inquiries.

When the conversation begins, give the speaker the opportunity to elaborate on her topic by asking reflective questions.

I thought I used advanced listening skills by asking probing questions, which made many of my athletes shrink away from me. They felt violated, pierced, poked and intimidated. When Rachel said, "Coach, I feel homesick," I asked, "What is causing your homesickness? Are you missing your parents, friends or your sisters?" (Not only did I probe; I gave her the answers. Apparently, I possessed the supernatural coaching powers of mind reading!)

Rachel answered, "Yeah, I guess that is it. I miss them."

I then offered advice and wisdom leaving poor Rachel without the ability to speak her truths.

Imagine now if I had said, "So, you feel homesick?" By asking a reflective question, I left Rachel the space to tell me more, and then allowed silence to fill the space between us and waited.

Rachel responded, "Yeah, I miss my teammates. They were such good friends of mine."

I could have gone off on a tangent here, but in this imaginary scenario, I was much wiser and said, "You enjoyed playing with your friends at home?" Again I remained silent and left her space.

"Yeah. They were more supportive. They cheered me on and wanted me to do well, not like the teammates I have now."

BINGO! I learned something I would have never learned if I had started with the probing questions. Now I could continue with the reflective questions or I could do a little more probing. Once the real issue is on the table, you have the option of asking more intimate questions.

In order to do this, you have to be present, *really* present. Your mind has to be focused on what the speaker is saying, and what she is trying to convey to you. You nod and make empathetic sounds to let her know you are listening, and when she is done speaking, you allow silence to hang between you. This shows you are not in a hurry to take over the conversation and that your ego does not need to speak.

Have you ever had a conversation where you kept the focus on the other person and only asked questions which reflected back to her feelings? If you haven't listened in this manner, then you haven't really been present for her, and you might have come away from the conversation only knowing what you know. Nothing has altered as a result of the conversation.

If you view each conversation as an opportunity for enrichment, then maybe you will be able to take yourself out of the equation. When you can let the other person do most of the talking and keep the focus on allowing her to discover her own answers, you keep your ego out of the conversation. As a result both of you will benefit.

Why are conversations so important? They are important because they define the relationship. Relationships can't occur without communication. Each opportunity to connect with another person is the relationship. Through conscious conversations we determine how other people relate to us and how we relate to ourselves. Word by word we create our connections, and our connections define our happiness and success.

DIALING INTO LISTENING

"So when you are listening to somebody, completely, attentively, then you are listening not only to the words, but also to the feeling of what is being conveyed, to the whole of it, not part of it."
—*Jiddu Krishnamurti*

My mother and father practiced selective listening, often leading to arguments which could have been avoided if they would have taken the time to hear one another. They often said the same thing in different way, but since neither of them was listening, they couldn't hear what was being said. Isn't this true of most disagreements—it is merely a lack of communication?

This joke illustrates the issue we have with listening.

I think my wife's going deaf," Joe told their doctor.

"Try to test her hearing at home and let me know how severe her problem is before you bring her in for treatment," the doctor said.

So that evening, when his wife was preparing dinner, Joe stood 15 feet behind her and said, "What's for dinner, honey?"

No response.

He moved to ten feet behind her and asked again.

No response.

Then he stood five feet in back of her and tried again but still got no answer. Finally, he stood directly behind her and asked,

"Honey, what's for supper?"

She turned around. "For the fourth time—I said chicken!"

Are you guilty of pretending to listen or blaming others for their inability to communicate? How many times have you nodded your head, responded with "That's nice," and never heard a word? How has this affected your relationships?

What if one of my parents had listened? If my father had heard my mother or vice versa, they might have laughed at the absurdity of their words rather than engage in a fight which left them angry for hours.

Here is a typical situation between my parents.

My mother is in the kitchen cooking. She has two pots on the stove and chicken baking in the oven. The phone is cradled between her ear and shoulder. Between stirring pots on the stove and talking on the phone, she fills the dishwasher up with dirty glasses and plates.

My father walks in the door, takes one look at the mess in the kitchen, and says, "Hey honey. Did you forget we were going out to eat tonight with the Pattersons?"

Mom nods her head and continues stirring and talking on the phone.

He turns his back to her and turns on the television set as he says, "We've got reservations at the new steak place downtown."

Mom puts her hand over the receiver as she says, "Dinner for the kids will be done by 7:00. I'll be ready after that."

He shakes his head as he watches the weather forecast on TV, "I don't know why you insist on eating before we go out. We can afford the steaks."

She opens the oven, tests the chicken and then looks at the clock. "I'll have everything ready so we can go."

Dad puts his hands on his hips. "I'm not going out to eat with the Pattersons if we are eating here first."

Mom mumbles something into the phone and mouths, "Don't worry. Dinner will be cooked and I'll be ready."

"I can't believe you. You make all this mess when you know I like to be on time. I try to do something nice for you, and you screw it up."

Mom hangs up the phone. "Why are you angry? I said I would be ready."

"Look at the mess you've made. You'll never be ready in time."

"If I didn't make this mess, your children wouldn't eat. Do you not care about your children?"

My father stomps out of the room while my mother throws a dishtowel at the pots on the stove.

In this scenario, my parents were not present for the conversation. They got angry over nothing. If either one of them would have stopped what they were doing, been present and asked questions for clarification, the issue would have been cleared up in one minute.

While you cannot control how the other person communicates or listens, you have the ability to change how your relationships are defined by dialing in and listening to the other person.

You improve your listening skills by becoming aware of how you listen or how you don't listen. When you are involved in a conversation, dedicate yourself to hear what the other person says, give your full attention, stop whatever you are doing, and eliminate distractions.

Listen with your eyes and not just your ears. People can misdirect with their words but most of the time they struggle keeping their body language from revealing how they feel. Notice if they continually avert their eyes, which means they are uncomfortable with the subject. They might show tension by rubbing their eyes or forehead. They might also use their body language to block you by crossing their arms.

Allow other people to finish their sentences, even if you know what they are going to say. Let them complete their thoughts. They will appreciate this small gesture, because they will feel your patience. Your listening skills indicate their words are valuable.

If they are angry and venting, allow them to vent. Give them time to wind down with their venting before you attempt to say anything. Many times when a person can get the words out, part of the anger is lost with the release of their thoughts.

Listening is a skill. It helps you gain information, understand others, improve your relationships, build commitments, and effectively handle complaints. When people feel understood, they are more willing to trust you. Trust is the number one indicator of positive outcomes in business as well as personal endeavors.

YOUR CHOICE—
THE CONVERSATION OR THE BREAKDOWN

The problem with communication is that most people are afraid to have honest communications. When we fail to have honest communications, breakdowns are guaranteed to occur. Because we struggle dealing with people in a straight and forward manner, whatever we fail to confront is guaranteed to not only show up, but multiply twofold.

It is challenging to confront people, because we fear the responses we might get. We fear that others will:

- Get defensive.

- Become angry, irrational, illogical, or depressed.

- Self-destruct.

- Decline to listen.

- Refuse to interact.

- Get even.

All of these reasons are true, and most of them will happen. But that does not give you a reason to allow a person's behavior to stop you from having a much needed conversation. Here is a question to ask yourself: Are you willing to let a dysfunctional person determine how you run you, your family or your company?

One of the teams I coached had five amazing players, three of whom were challenging to coach. All three of them were stuck in victimhood, blaming everybody else for their emotional responses to the world. When I confronted them, I got their blowback— anger, curse words, accusations of unfairness, the silent treatment, and threats to quit.

I spent a majority of my time on two of them, talking to them, disciplining them, and offering a listening ear. One of the players, I will call her "E," listened the least. Because of this, I let her actions slide the most. When I failed to correctly praise her during a film session, she threw a temper tantrum. When I did not slap her hand when she came out of the game for a brief rest, she refused to play hard when she went back into the game. It didn't matter to her if I was in the midst of calling a play or having a chat with another player, everything should stop for her. I allowed her actions to continue, because talking to her was uncomfortable for me.

Because I failed to confront her, the last game of the season ended in a catastrophe. We were playing in the semi-finals of the conference tournament. Despite our 23-7 record, we needed to win the game in order to advance to the national tournament. Our seniors, feeling a tremendous amount of pressure, choked and played horribly. We were down by 20 points when I substituted the bench players in for the starters.

When I took "E" out of the game, she threw a class one temper tantrum. I made her sit down on the bench. Soon I heard her yelling at my assistant coach, "Let's take this outside—you and me."

I ran down the bench and said, "You are done. Go to the locker room."

Through the slits of her black eyes, she glared at me defiantly, "You can't make me."

I was so taken aback by her response that I didn't know what to say. She was right. I actually didn't have the physical power to make her go to the locker room. If I touched her, I would be the one reprimanded. So I responded with as much muster as I could, "You will not go back into the game. You are done."

"I will play if I want to."

Over my dead body I thought, but I didn't know how I could stop her from going in the game. If she jogged toward the scorer's table and I physically grabbed her, I could get in trouble. What a nightmare!

"E" eventually made a huge show of grabbing her warm-ups and marching off to the locker room, but that wasn't the end of the story. She accused the coaching staff of saying things we didn't say; she rallied her teammates against us; and she even went to the president of the university to try to get us fired. It was a long and complicated mess which took two months to resolve.

Yet, I wasn't angry at her; I was **upset** with myself. It was my fault. I failed to have the honest and tough conversations I should have had with her. She was simply behaving in the ways I allowed her to behave.

One of the reasons it is so challenging for us to have honest conversations is because we are taught to be nice, to not hurt somebody's feelings, and to sugarcoat our feedback. The truth is we can still be nice if we are having the conversations that are needed without bringing our emotions and ego into those conversations. In fact, when we allow ourselves to provide the truth in a factual manner, we give a gift to the other person. We provide that person an opportunity to make a change for the better.

If I would have had authentic conversations with "E," she might have changed. She might have had more respect for the coaching staff, or I might have cut her from the team. But the fact is she wouldn't have run the team through her dysfunction.

If you are not yet convinced that genuine conversations are needed, think about a time in your life where you wished somebody would have been honest with you. You believe if somebody else had told you the truth, it would have spared you further pain. Yet, when it comes to us having that same conversation for other people it feels so difficult, because we are afraid of the other person's reactions.

Our fear stops us from living our integrity and from doing our jobs.

How do you start having the conversations that you need? You begin by having the awareness that what you don't deal with doesn't go away; it gets bigger. Once you understand that fact, the next step is to get beyond your fear by having a method you can utilize for tough conversations.

Here are some simple steps to follow when you know that a tough conversation is needed:

1. Put your ego aside, which means having the conversation without using blame, guilt, or intimidation methods.

2. Go into the conversation with the idea you want to resolve the issue by allowing both of you a chance to evolve.

3. Be able to put a name and a face to the issue. Be clear and exact about the reasons for the conversation.

4. Provide a specific example of their inappropriate behavior.

5. Spell out exactly what is at stake. Let them know what happens if they do change and what happens if they fail to change.

6. Specify your desire to solve this issue.

7. Give them an opportunity to respond. This should be the heart of the conversation.

8. Listen with your ears and your eyes. Ask questions. Discover the why beneath their behavior.

9. Come to an agreement. Decide upon a course of action.

When you spend the time to have honest conversations, you show respect for others and respect for yourself. These conversations allow you and the people you care about to evolve. You solve complicated issues before they become major problems. You emerge as the person who has the ability to meet challenges and take yourself and others to higher levels of success.

By improving your communication skills, you alter your life. You create better relationships by avoiding the murky waters of misunderstanding. You increase your integrity by feeling good about how you handle confrontations and how you speak to others in a way which builds them up rather than tears them down. You walk away from every conversation knowing you brought a gift of honesty and compassion through your words. You help others feel better about themselves while enhancing your self-confidence.

EXAMINE AND CHANGE YOUR COMMUNICATION SKILLS

1. Practice listening for three days. Listen with both your eyes and ears. Don't offer advice, share stories or judge the people you listen to. Ask them clarifying or reflective questions. Write down your observations at the end of the third day. What did you learn?

2. Take the Maggie Challenge. Listen to your negative self talk for an entire day. Say "I release this thought and replace it with love." Release any talk which could be construed as negative—complaining, whining, what-if-down thinking, judging, etc.

3. Determine one person who you need to have an honest conversation with and give yourself a timeline for that conversation. Keep your integrity in place during the conversation. Allow the other person to respond without taking it personally. Come to an agreement.

4. Write down five examples of how you didn't allow somebody to challenge you. It could be your children, your parents or a co-worker. What methods did you use to make certain you wouldn't be challenged?

5. Listen to how you offer feedback. Do you use the contrary contraction "But?" For the next week, practice using the cooperative conjunction "And."

6. Ask ten people who you trust to evaluate your communication skills. Ask:

   a. What do you feel like when I offer constructive feedback?

   b. Does my feedback come across as instructive and helpful?

   c. Do you feel comfortable having conversations about tough topics with me? Why or why not?

   d. How can I improve my listening skills? Do I have open body language and good eye contact? Do I interrupt when you are talking? Do I ask you pertinent questions?

e. If you could change one thing about my communication skills, what would it be?

f. How am I receptive to constructive feedback?

g. Do I avoid having tough conversations? If so, provide an example.

CHAPTER FOUR

NOURISH
YOURSELF

ALLOW YOURSELF TO GROW

GIVE YOURSELF PERMISSION

Why is it we believe in the idea of service, yet we refuse to believe in servicing ourselves? We suffer from the conviction that giving to ourselves is selfish. It is egotistical. It makes us arrogant, cruel and conceited.

We are often provided with instructions from our mentors that when we think of ourselves first we are not doing our part in the universe. If you are a teacher, you might have heard the phrase, "You don't do this for the money; you do it for the kids." As a coach, I heard, "You coach for the love of coaching kids, not for the salary."

Part of what we do is give to others. It is what creates the ability for society to function as a whole, but should we feel guilty when we have the desire to receive as well as give? Receiving is not immoral. After all who would be the recipient if we all gave? There has to be both in order for balance to occur.

To truly comprehend giving; shouldn't you first experience it? How can you give unconditional love without first having experienced loving yourself unconditionally? You can only offer a partial gift when you don't fully grasp the gift you offer. Wouldn't it be better to first live love, to feel the beauty of inner self, and to connect with all that is joy before trying to offer it?

Gretchen Rubin, author of *The Happiness Project: Or Why I Spent a Year Trying to Sing in the Morning, Clean My Closets, Fight Right, Read Aristotle, and Generally Have More Fun* said, "The belief that unhappiness is selfless and happiness is selfish is misguided. It's more selfless to act happy. It takes energy, generosity, and discipline to be unfailingly lighthearted, yet everyone takes the happy person for granted. No one is careful of his feelings or tries to keep his spirits high. He seems self-sufficient; he becomes a cushion for others. And because happiness seems unforced, that person usually gets no credit."

The power comes from giving to yourself unselfishly and then having done so, sharing your knowledge, compassion and happiness with others. You do not have to sacrifice your peace; because you are living so completely in harmony with peace that it freely leaves you and attaches to those surrounding you.

A coaching client of mine, Jamie, struggled with giving herself permission to take time to exercise, something which made her happy. She felt guilty taking an hour for herself when her clients needed her during the day, and she couldn't bear to take time in the evening away from her children and husband. Because she wasn't taking time to nourish herself, she was angry. The nourishment she denied herself led her to becoming angry at those around her for not allowing her to do what she loved. This denial leaked out to her husband when he failed to take out the garbage, to her children when they fought amongst themselves, and to her clients when they called to reschedule an appointment.

She was taught to neglect what nourished her so that she could nourish others. Who suffered? Everybody. This is what happens when we fail to nourish ourselves. We can't help others because we suffer too much internally to get outside of ourselves.

BECOME A LEARN-IT-ALL

We only know what we know; therefore, we limit ourselves to our past experiences. During the early stages of my chronic pain, I reverted back to what I'd been taught about injuries and pain. When I was five and broke my leg, my mother took me to the doctor to get a cast on it. When I dislocated my index finger during a softball game, I drove myself to the emergency room to get it set. When I had a temperature of 104, I went to the doctor for medicine. This was all I knew.

After a month of chronic pain, I scheduled a visit to the doctor where I believed he would prescribe medication or surgery, and I'd be done with it. My view became stretched as I went to doctor after doctor after doctor without any answers. I went to back specialists, physical therapists, chiropractors, acupuncturists, and massage therapists. I had cat scans, bone scans, MRI's, and just about every test known to mankind. If one specialist didn't have an answer, I went to another one. I knew somebody had to have an answer.

After two years without relief or a diagnosis beyond the generic formula of chronic pain, I was stumped. The doctors, those individuals who studied 8-10 years to know the answers, couldn't offer any answers either. The doctors' solution was for me to attend a pain management clinic where I would learn how to manage the pain. I didn't accept their solution so I kept looking.

What I discovered about doctors is they only know what they know. They learn within their system and then teach from that system. Does it mean doctors are wrong? No. They know their system well, and their system sometimes works. When doctors fail is when their system doesn't work and they accept failure as the final answer.

There is no final answer. There is only another question. If we don't have the right answer, we haven't asked the right question.

The way to become completely nourished is to continue the quest to become a Learn-It-All, which means you focus on asking the right questions and looking for the answers. You might not be aware of what the right questions are, but you continue to seek them to expand who you are.

I continued asking questions about my health for 19 years. In fact, I'm still asking questions. Due to my persistence, I found many different answers. Some answers worked better than others, which is why I am still on the quest. I learned information I questioned as viable at the beginning of my journey:

- Pain or disease is not due to physical factors only.

- The body is connected to the spirit and the mind, so what affects the mind or spirit also affects the body.

- Negative energy can be stored in the body. That stored energy disrupts the natural flow of energy.

- The body cannot heal itself when there is disruption in the flow of energy.

I refused to accept what my doctors understood as truth, because their options gave me no hope. Hope was needed to survive the physical pain which was so intense daily chores were impossible.

Due to the intensity of the pain, I plotted ways to escape, and one of my plots involved suicide. I persisted in my search for answers, because I had been taught as an athlete to play through pain. I also believed there were answers out there somewhere even if I didn't know where that somewhere was. I nourished myself by continuing to look for answers and having the faith there were answers.

HOW DO YOU ACCESS MORE INFORMATION?

Many people have the illusion they know enough—they have a college degree, job training and life experiences. They possess the answers to paying the mortgage and saving for retirement. Like teenagers they arrive at a place where they think they know enough and more than most people. This is an illusion of knowledge—they are in unconscious incompetence falling short of living in self awareness.

Socrates said, "The only true wisdom is in knowing you know nothing."

Einstein said, "The only thing that interferes with my learning is my education."

Take a few minutes to surf the internet or go to the library to count all the books you haven't read. You have so much more to learn that it is impossible for you to learn it all in this lifetime. You could read every day for ten hours a day and barely scratch the surface of knowledge. Even as you read, there are new ideas being tested, theories being formed, and technology being built.

Our thirst for knowledge triggers our evolution to higher levels of awareness. My thirst for knowledge altered my life. Through knowledge I was able to return to moving, running, hiking and playing. My quest gave me laughter and insight, love and forgiveness. Without the drive for wisdom I would have remained the miserable young woman of 20 who believed the world was her enemy.

The ability to grow is at our finger tips. *We make the decision every day to nourish ourselves or to deny ourselves.*

Dave Anderson, owner of Famous Dave's Barbeque Restaurants, spoke at a James Malinchak Seminar in December of 2013. At the time he was worth 500 million dollars and owned over 179 restaurants. He said the secret to his success was reading two-three hours per day. He changed his life by his willingness to be a Learn-It-All. He was a below average student in high school earning C's, D's and F's and was destined for a life of mediocrity until he had the opportunity to meet Zig Ziglar. Zig became his mentor, and the one lesson Zig pounded into Dave's head was the importance of lifelong learning.

This is the secret to your success: NOURISH YOURSELF THROUGH LIFELONG LEARNING.

1. Set aside time every day to read. Make it a habit. Put it on your list of things to accomplish daily. Ask people the titles for the best books they've read. Make a list of them. Read them one by one. Make it a goal to read a book per week. Read books outside of your comfort zone. Stretch your knowledge and your imagination.

2. If you don't like to read, do it anyway. The more you read, the more you will like reading.

3. If you prefer listening to audio, use your car as a university. Learn something every day while you drive back and forth to work. Turn on an audio book

when you clean dishes or cook. Turn off the television at night so you can listen or read something which expands your mind.

4. Go to seminars. Listen for the one piece of information you don't know.

5. Hire a personal coach. Hire somebody who can help you see what you cannot recognize in yourself. Be coachable and listen.

6. Keep a notebook. Jot down things you've learned or quotes you like. Write your thoughts. Once you've listened and then written your thoughts down, you are more likely to retain them.

7. Become a teacher. When you teach what you know, you really learn it.

8. Establish or join a group of people whose quest is personal development.

9. AND listen. Ask questions. Keep asking questions. Listen to the answer even if you don't agree with it. Question why you disagree. Keep your mind open to possibilities rather than fighting for what you believe you know.

NOURISHMENT FOR YOUR EMOTIONS, BODY AND SPIRIT

FOOD IS MORE THAN FUEL

I grew up with a mother who hated her body. I observed as she took diet pills, tried one diet after another, and lamented about how fat she was. The more she focused on what she didn't want, the more weight she gained.

I followed in her footsteps accepting her blueprint for viewing my body as fat. I didn't want to be fat, so I denied myself food. I thought food was the culprit, and it is…but it isn't. Food was essential to my health, but my blueprint taught me that food was evil. If I didn't have the mindset food was the culprit, I wouldn't have reduced my caloric intake to 1200 calories a day when I was training twice a day for the Olympics. Can you imagine how my body used muscle to train, because it wasn't getting enough protein? This low caloric intake actually created thyroid problems for me in my 40's.

What actions we take now have an effect on us later in life. We create our future by our choices today.

When we drop our caloric count too low, it causes our bodies to adapt to the threat of starvation. This stress involves interaction with our thyroid hormone, which regulates our metabolism. This master hormone affects other glands as well. It plays an active role in the production of proteins, the decomposing of fat, and the regulation of temperature.

The thyroid doesn't stop there. When it is underactive, it leads to a host of problems such as depression, infertility issues, fatigue, dry skin, hair loss, brain fog, and weight gain. So my determination to lose weight through extreme dieting actually caused reduced thyroid function, which in turn created a slower metabolism and weight gain.

There are many other issues associated with poor nutrition. There are physical problems associated with lack of protein, lack of vitamins and minerals, and too much sugar in the diet. Aids and cancer have been linked to a lack of protein. Not enough vitamins and minerals can result in several different diseases such as joint pain, bone-softening, spongy gums, weakness, weight loss, and emotional disturbances. An increase in processed sugar in the diet is linked to an increase in obesity, high blood pressure, and deadly heart problems.

Many of our health issues are linked to improper nutrition. What we eat and how much we eat not only affects our long term health; it affects our emotions and ability to think. Ask any diabetic what happens to her ability to think logically when her blood sugar drops. Ask any overweight person how challenging it is to get in and out of a car or an airplane and how that affects the way she feels about herself. Ask any anorexic how difficult it is to enjoy outdoor activities with her family.

For most of my teenage years and early twenties I struggled with severe mood swings. Even when I knew I was being irrational, I couldn't stop myself. I thought I was crazy, bordering on the edge of insanity, because I had no ability to control my emotions. I felt like I had PMS 24 hours a day, seven days a week.

When I was 27, several of my Olympic teammates decided to give up something they cherished for Lent. Even though I wasn't Catholic, I decided to see if I could give up sweets for 40 days. Within one week I noticed a change in my ability to control emotions. After 30 days I was no longer irrational. It didn't take me long to connect the dots. By giving up sugar I gained control over my emotional lows and was back in charge of my life.

How you nourish your body is important to maintaining a healthy weight, increased longevity, and positive mental health. Nourish yourself through proper nutrition so you won't suffer tomorrow for what you are doing to your body today.

EXERCISE: THE NOURISHMENT FOR THE BODY

Our personal house consists of the mind, the body and the spirit. Each of these aspects is a foundation for how strong our house stands. By neglecting one of these aspects, our foundation becomes weakened. *Our body is not separate from our mind, or our mind separate from our spirit, nor our spirit separate from our body. We are a unit. The strength of each one of these parts creates a better whole.*

Our physical pain has often been separated from our emotional pain by medical practitioners. They were taught to look at the science of the body. How often have you gone to the doctor to complain of a physical ailment and the doctor responded by asking what was going on in your personal life? Probably not very often. Yet, you've probably felt a physical pain in your body when you've experienced a traumatic loss like a divorce, the death of a loved one, or the loss of a job. If you were heartbroken over the loss of a partner, your chest might have felt like it was a vacuum sucking life out of you.

Each piece of us affects the rest of us.

We cannot separate our torso from our legs and keep walking, and we can't separate our body from our mind pretending we are healthy. We need to exercise our minds, our bodies and our spirit. Each of these requires attention in order to keep the foundation of our physical home healthy.

John J. Ratey, MD, author of *A User's Guide to the Brain*, said "Exercise is really for the brain, not the body. It affects mood, vitality, alertness, and feelings of well-being."

Exercise pumps more oxygen to the brain, stimulating brain plasticity by linking the growth of new neuronal connections, and aids in the release of varied hormones which provide a nourishing environment for the evolution of brain cells. Exercise assists with memory and learning and keeps the brain healthier. Exercise also releases serotonin and dopamine which make us feel cheerful and blissful.

One of my former athletes, Laura Kinsler, became a physician's assistant. I asked Laura, "What is the most important lesson you gained from nine years of college classes?"

Laura said, "There are three things people need to do and almost all of their physical issues will go away: eat right, get enough sleep, and exercise. If we could prescribe these three things and people would do them, 90% of all ailments would be cured."

At the 1988 Olympic Games, I learned the connection to body and spirit. My Olympic coach cornered me in an elevator, pressed his pelvis into mine and shoved his tongue deep into my mouth. He told me, "I dream of seeing you naked all night." His continued sexual encroachments created hell for me, because I didn't feel like I had any alternatives. If I said, "No" to his sexual overtures, he might decide to bench me.

Every time he mouthed, "I want you," I wanted to punch him. I couldn't stand to hear his voice when he coached me. The more he winked at me, kissed me and told me of his desire for my body, the more belligerent I became on the court. The situation ended with me being kicked out of my final Olympic team handball game by the president of the United States Team Handball Federation.

After the Olympics were over, I was supposed to assume duties as assistant coach for the national team. Two months later I was fired by the team handball executive board for insubordination (i.e. reporting the sexual harassment). I filed with the Office of Civil Rights for illegal termination. The lawyers from the team handball federation came back with a vengeance reporting every misstep I had ever taken as a player. They were prepared to dismantle me.

I fell into deep depression. Life as I knew it was over. The 21 years I spent dreaming and then training for the Olympics was gone. Retiring as an athlete would have been enough to send me spiraling into depression, but to be ignored, fired and accused of lying was, in my mind, worse than death. I had nothing—no job, no salary, no savings, and no place to live because I was evicted from the Olympic Training Center.

Life was bleak. I couldn't see any possibility. There was no reason to train. No reason to run, to lift weights or to sweat. No reason to get up out of bed when the day offered me nothing except emptiness.

If I would have had more money, I would have drunk myself into oblivion. Instead I curled up in the top room of a friend's house and hid beneath the sheets. My irrational thinking was that if I hid long enough I would disappear. I daydreamed about hiking up Pike's Peak, the fourteen foot mountain which loomed just outside my window, lying down in the snow and freezing to death. That way nobody would find me until spring or maybe they would never find me. I would fade away to nothingness.

My friend, Taina, exasperated with my moping said, "Sherry, go outside. Go for a run. Move. Let your muscles feel again. You've always loved working out. Go. Give yourself something you love."

Fearful of imposing too much on Taina and having her evict me too, I determined to give my best effort to run. I wrapped myself up in sweats, gloves and a jacket and took off running at a snail's pace in the December wind. My legs were like wine kegs, heavy and saturated with aged anger. My feet were like corks, stiff and stopping all the earth's natural energy from moving into me. Step by step I forced myself to lean into the biting wind, to feel the slap of the cold air on my cheeks. Cursing the wind, the cold, and myself, I turned left and ran into the Garden of the Gods, a public park known for the formation of its red rocks which perched like ancient gods in the mountains.

As I ran and looked at the beauty surrounding me, my legs and feet became lighter. My body seemed to float on the road, and something strange grabbed me. It was a smile. Hope was alive inside me. The more I ran the three mile loop, the more the smile widened throughout my body. The running wasn't a panacea for all my emotional pain, but I acknowledged possibility beyond the pain. My spirits lifted, supplying me with enough energy to leave my self-imposed prison. I returned to college, completed my Master's Degree and a year later was hired to coach women's basketball at the University of Minnesota-Morris.

NOURISHMENT FOR THE SPIRIT

You can add a dose of fish oil in the morning with your green tea to help supplement your nutrition, and you can add a 30 minute walk in the evening to exercise your body, but what do you add to nourish your spirit? Nourishing the spirit seems like a more arduous task, but is it?

In 2009 when I was coaching at the University of Charleston, I struggled with balancing the different parts of my life. It seemed all I did was work. I told my athletic director I was giving a gallon of myself every day and getting a shot glass back for my efforts. He laughed and said, "When you are a coach, it is not a job or a career; it is a lifestyle. It is not what you do; it is who you are all the time."

I walked out of his office more dispirited than ever. I couldn't keep giving of myself until there was nothing left. I needed to refill my spirit but I wasn't certain how to go about it. How did I fill myself with the necessary ingredients to feel energized and inspired? I wanted inspiration which ignited me and propelled me to establish new goals and to feel the same fire I had as a child when I believed all dreams were possible.

I wanted a child's innocent enthusiasm for miracles.

I had forgotten how to see possibilities through a child's eyes. I trudged through life rather than danced and was tainted with my perception of reality. There was no Easter Bunny, no Santa Claus, no Miracle on 34th Street, no Polar Bear Express, no magical wand, no Superman or Batman, and no magical clicking of heels in ruby shoes. Life had lost its wonder for me.

I needed to shift out of this mindset. I needed a new me, but how did I shed the skin of old thinking to reemerge as somebody new?

I told my chiropractor my symptoms—apathy, lethargy, and weariness. He said, "What do you to fill your spirit?"

"I read some personal development books. I exercise."

"Do you dream?"

"Of course. I usually don't remember them. Sometimes I do right when I wake up."

He shook his head. "No, I meant do you daydream? Do you dream of things you want to accomplish?"

I thought about it. "No. I guess not. I think I've spent all my energy on two things: one is getting healthy, something I've been working on for 13 years, and the other one is coaching."

He said, "Here is what I do every day. I read something spiritual. I meditate. I spend a few minutes being grateful, and then I take a walk and look for something beautiful I haven't noticed before. Then I dream about whom I want to become and what I want to do. I let myself live in that dream as I walk."

I departed his office thinking more about his question. I didn't dream anymore. Dreams were too demanding and they were illusionary. Being healthy had been my main agenda for so long that nothing besides work could even edge its way into my brain. I had quit believing in dreams. There were no goals which tantalized me. I was simply existing and doing what I promised I'd never do again—surviving rather than living my life.

My days lacked mystery; I made hours bland, mundane and ordinary. I had lost my charisma—the sparkle in my eyes and the pep in my step. I was in survival mode, doing the necessary deeds and taking the required steps to make it through each day.

I needed inspiration. My spirit required resuscitation so I could breathe life back into dreaming.

Where I should begin? The answer: Where I was. But I didn't have to stay there.

I listened to the wisdom my chiropractor offered and began creating time to nourish my spirit in the morning before going to work. Here are the things I changed:

✓ Reading for 10-15 minutes from a spiritual book.
  I define spiritual as being a book which energizes and

comes from the place of peace, joy, harmony and love.

✓ Listening to an audio book or a recorded webinar which infused me with motivation while I cooked breakfast.

✓ Spending 5-20 minutes in meditation.

✓ Walking my dogs for 20 minutes. During this time I practiced an attitude of gratitude. I allowed myself to stop and watch a leaf as it danced to the ground, a raindrop hover on a flower petal, or any act of nature which I hadn't seen with fresh eyes.

✓ Reciting my affirmations and blessing my co-workers and team on the 20 minute drive to work.

I could not define exactly what I was searching for, but knew when I found it I would know. Then one day I read this quote from Dr. Wayne Dyer and understood.

**"Once you believe in yourself
and see your soul as divine and precious,
you'll automatically be converted
to a being who can create miracles."**

All the work I was doing was to remember who I really was. I was a miracle.

There are many ways to reconnect with the spirit within you and to re-remember who you are and what precious abilities you hold. As you nourish your soul, you will feel infused with something far beyond what you have known and will connect with all things. This connection will tether you to the creator that you are.

LAUGHTER AS A DOSE OF NOURISHMENT

"The human race has one really
effective weapon, and that is laughter."
— Mark Twain

Stress is known as a primary cause for almost every ailment there is. Scientists have indicated stress is a factor in food cravings, obesity, heart attacks, insomnia, headaches, hair loss, blood sugar, blood pressure, brain tissue, back pain, stroke, colds, asthma, seizures, and sex drive.

According to Robert Sapolsky, PhD, and author of *Why Zebras Don't Get Ulcers*, we face vastly different stressors today than our ancestors did. Our ancestors used their flight or fight response for the purposes of evolution. If they were stalked by a predator, the stress was intense, short-lived and obvious. Our ancestors ran, fought or died. The cause of their stress ended rather quickly.

Our stressors today are diverse, ongoing and lingering. Our stress is more likely to look like an incompetent boss, traffic jam, or financial challenges—things which don't appear significant when contrasted to life or death. The lasting effect of these constant stressors still triggers a flood of chemicals that shuts down important but not urgent survival functions. Our body shuts down the less urgent functions like digestion, growth and emotional bonding to support reactions like enhanced focus, quicker reaction times, and greater energy bursts which are designed to help us get through a short-term crisis.

In the long term, the oversupply of cortisol and adrenaline we use to combat stress, wreaks havoc on our bodies and minds. This chronic stress is the stress which creates our health issues.

Laughter, on the other hand, is one of the answers to stress. What does laughter do?

Laughter releases physical tension allowing our muscles to relax up to 45 minutes after having a good hearty guffaw. It boosts the immune system by decreasing stress hormones and increasing immune cells and infection-fighting antibodies. It triggers the release of endorphins which promote a sense of well-being, and it improves the function of our hearts by increasing blood flow and improving the function of blood vessels.

When was the last time you allowed yourself to laugh, really laugh, the kind of laughter where your cheeks ached and your stomach hurt, where you laid on the ground and kicked your feet in the air? If you can't remember the last time you laughed like this, it has been too long.

One of my goals was to make my players laugh every day on the basketball court. When the players laughed together, they played better as a unit. The players' laughter released self-imposed pressure and allowed them to associate hard work with fun. When a particularly stressful opponent was on the schedule, I often had my athletes play a silly game before practice. We might play stack tag, a hysterical game which often led to belly laughs. My other favorite game was Whozit, a guessing game which involved imitating one another. Many of the athletes found joy in imitating me. Apparently I was the cause of an enormous amount of laughter in the dorm rooms.

About two or three times a year, my pregame speech would involve a joke with the intention of lightening the mood. There were even times during games when I called time out to tell the players a joke, and then sent them back into the game with no further instructions.

One particular game I almost got thrown out of the game, because the NCAA officials thought I was berating my players when my objective was to make them laugh. It was the halftime of the first game of the 2006 NCAA East Regional Championships, which meant it was do-or-die for the teams. The losers went home while the winners continued to the next round. Because we were ranked number one in the region, we hosted the tournament at our gym, which created more angst for the team. They wanted to perform their best in front of their friends and home crowd fans.

As number one seed, we were matched against the number eight seed, a team we had beaten early in the season by 25 points. It should have been an easy game, but we allowed the perception of pressure to get to us. By halftime, my All-American and leader of the team had thrown a major temper tantrum as we stumbled and bumbled our way into a five point deficit. My players acted as if we had already lost the game even though 20 minutes remained on the clock for the second half.

My objective at half-time was to get the team to relax. I made fun of myself, joked about how we couldn't make a lay-up, and then said, "There is only one team who has the talent to beat us in this tournament, and you are looking at that team. No other team possesses your skills. You are the best."

When I walked out of the locker room to watch us warm up for the second half, I saw their slack faces and limp body language. I knew we were going to lose the game unless I did something drastic.

I didn't formulate a plan before I ran out onto the court in front of 3,000 fans. I just acted. I screamed and yelled, chest-bumped, and high-fived my players. I got nothing. Not even a flicker of a smile from the team. I searched for a method to get them to switch their energy and reached a little deeper in the recesses of my mind. I yelled, "DOWN" which was my signal for them to do a frozen push-up.

During practices, we had emphasis drills. When the players failed to complete the emphasis of the drill, they did a frozen push-up, which was prefaced by me yelling, "Down." I then proliferated for 30-55 seconds on why they should do the particular skill in the way we required them to do it. In this manner, I gained their attention and made them focus on skill techniques. The frozen push-up method was for practice emphasis and had never been used in game situations.

The players looked at the fans in the stands, and then they looked at me for confirmation. I barked, "DOWN." Once they got into their frozen push-up, I yelled, "You are the best team here. There is only one team who can beat you and that is you. This is your court—your place of victory. You have the talent. You have the team. You have the coach. What you don't have right now is faith in yourselves." I continued screaming and repeating the winning concepts.

The players' arms started to shake. Their faces turned red. And then, the unthinkable happened. A player gave out. She plopped onto the floor like a high diver hitting the water with a belly flop. Her teammates gasped and held their collective breaths looking for my reaction.

In practice if a team member failed to hold her frozen push-up, I would have gone ballistic making all of them get back into the frozen push-up until their bodies gave out, and then I would have made them do it again and maybe even again.

But this time I laughed. Just laughed. They looked at me, hesitated for a moment, and then all of them belly flopped to the floor and began laughing.

When we got back into our huddle I said, "That is all you needed to do. Laugh. This is your game now. Go have fun."

They did and we won. The difference was in the laughter. It was the stress buster.

Laughter nourishes the soul. It refreshes the mind. It allows the growl to turn into a grin. It changes the dismal into the bright, and it gives the dreary a new coat of white.

AND it gives the team a chance to win.

HOW YOU THINK ABOUT YOURSELF REALLY MATTERS

WHO ARE YOU REALLY?

In January of 2014, I received two emails from high school friends who found me on the internet. I was relieved they had found me, because I wanted to apologize to both of them for whom I had been at the time of our friendship. I had fretted over, judged myself and berated myself so much about these events that I had lived in guilt for 35 years. Ironically, neither of my friends remembered the events the same way. Their memories were of fun times.

Judgments I had carried around for years had not even been noted in their memories.

Have you done the same thing to yourself? Have you starved yourself of forgiveness because of past judgments?

Nothing really matters except how we think about ourselves, because everybody else's opinion of us is fleeting. Their opinion of us is gone within minutes because they are busy thinking about how they fit into the picture. Like us, they can't stop thinking about themselves.

This is why our thoughts about who we are really matter. They matter to us because we become who we think we are. It doesn't matter what awards or recognitions we receive, because they don't change our perceptions of self. Only we can do that. We are responsible for nourishing ourselves. Nobody else can change what we hear or see in ourselves.

In 2009 when my University of Charleston Golden Eagles won the West Virginia Conference and the conference tournament, neither my players nor I were recognized by the conference coaches. I didn't get coach of the year, nor did one of my players receive player of the year. In fact, after we won the conference tournament, our opponents received the Heart and Hustle Award, the MVP, and three members on the all-tournament team. We got one player on the all-tournament team. My players were upset. The fans were livid.

I was disappointed but not mad. Why? Because the lack of recognition by others didn't change who we were or what we had accomplished. We were still the conference champions and the tournament champions. Having somebody else recognize our talents or not recognize them for whatever reasons couldn't change what we thought about ourselves. Being named coach of the year wouldn't have made me a better coach. It would have been nice to be recognized, but it wouldn't have changed what I believed about myself.

At the end of our lives, the plaques, the newspaper articles and the records we've achieved don't indicate who we are. Only we know our secrets. Only we know the things we did and said, the people we helped or hurt, and how far we took our talents. We are the ones who can offer ourselves forgiveness and unconditional love. Who knows what we deserve more than ourselves? We are the ones with the ultimate job of nourishing our successes and failures, and of valuing our growth.

STAY CONNECTED TO ALL OF YOU

Nourishing yourself means understanding the connection between you, your mind, your spirit, and your body. We are interconnected. We like to think we can disconnect pieces of ourselves, and sometimes we manage to do this for short periods of time. When we choose to do this, we suffer as a whole.

Maybe you've been told not to bring your troubles with you to work. As an athlete I was told by my coaches to leave my troubles off the court. I tried to disconnect pieces of me assigning some to stay home while I was on the court, but the problem was that those pieces never obeyed my commands. They lingered within me waiting for a time to pounce.

<u>What we deny comes back to us, because we never dealt with it in the first place</u>. We shoved it somewhere. It is like shoving a box of photographs under the bed. We momentarily forget about the box, but it is always there. The minute we open the box up, the memories come flooding back to us. We feel the emotions attached to the photographs: joy, sorrow, anguish, despair, distress, delight, happiness, pleasure, bliss, or elation.

Our teachers taught us the wrong lesson. We were taught not to cry, to be tough, to pull ourselves up by the bootstraps, and to pretend all was okay. We gutted it out. We swallowed our feelings so other people would be okay. We showed our resiliency, our ability to overcome, and we were rewarded by those around us for being strong in the face of adversity.

Being strong, resilient and loving your challenges are celebrated characteristics, but pretending not to feel your emotions is detrimental to your health. You nourish yourself through feeling your emotions. You don't deny them or push them away. You feel them. The very act of feeling an emotion dissipates it.

You are challenged by the day-to-day emotions which engulf you. Even if you believed being dumped by your partner was for your best emotional health, you would still feel the lingering emotions of unhappiness, loneliness or undesirability. Rather than push these emotions away, it is better to feel them and release them.

When you deny your emotions you allow them to attack you later.

In an article published in *Psychology Today*, June 2011, Nadja Geipert stated, "Years of research strongly suggest that emotions are adaptations that serve a fundamental purpose to our survival. We can't will them away anymore than the urge to eat or sleep. They inform us about what's good for us and what (or whom) we should steer clear off. And seriously, if we could will bad feelings away, wouldn't we all be doing it?"

Since our emotions provide essential information, wouldn't it be better to listen to the signals they are providing us?

The Sedona Method by Hale Dwoskin offers a very clear way to allow emotions to pass through us:

1.   Feel whatever you are feeling at the moment. Don't try to push it away or resist it. Just allow the emotion to

flow through you.

2. Ask yourself if you are willing to take action by either letting, allowing or welcoming the feeling. "Can I welcome this feeling?"

3. Can you release the emotion? "Am I willing to let it go?"

4. When will you let the emotion go? This is an invitation to let it go now. "When can I let this go?"

Asking the questions with awareness dissolves the intensity of the emotion. If your answer is "No" to any of the questions, go back through the process until you allow yourself to release the emotion.

When my response to a question is "No," I add the question, "Why am I unwilling to let this go?" When I can answer the why question, I work on releasing it. For example, I might ask, "Am I willing to welcome the feeling of being embarrassed right now?"

If I answer in the negative, I ask, "Why am I unwilling to release the feeling of being embarrassed?"

My answer, "If I release this feeling, I won't learn the lesson."

This is how my brain works. I need to keep the lesson so I won't do the same action again. I then ask, "Can I release the lesson?"

Usually, when I address the more specific reason, I can let it go. If I can't, I'll ask why again.

I continue releasing and asking why until the intensity of the emotion dissipates to where I no longer feel it is hampering me.

Our emotions are clues. They warn, prepare and stimulate us. When we ignore them, we ignore our internal warning signs. We starve our bodies of nourishment when we deny our emotions. By allowing a feeling to come and then to go, we accept it as part of who we are. This is part of unconditional love, connecting to our higher selves and nourishing our souls.

NOURISH YOURSELF THROUGH THESE SIMPLE ACTION STEPS

1. Write down five ways you deny yourself because you think you should spend that time nourishing others. What one activity you will give yourself permission to do that nourishes you?

2. How much time are you willing to dedicate to becoming a lifelong learner? What habit will you start tomorrow which will assure that you will always continue to learn?

3. List one method you will institute for each of these elements that will positively impact your future:

    a. Nutrition.

    b. Exercise.

    c. Spirit.

4. List ten ways you judge yourself which keeps you in guilt or shame.

5. Practice self-forgiveness for the ways you have judged yourself. For more help with self-forgiveness, Google Emotional Freedom Technique, the Sedona Method or Ho'oponono.

6. Make laughter a part of your day. Laugh by yourself or with others. It doesn't make any difference. If you haven't laughed, play a YouTube video of something funny.

CHAPTER FIVE

NURTURE ALL RELATIONSHIPS

DO MORE THAN CHEERLEAD

BE A YAYSAYER TO NURTURE POTENTIALITY

The value you bring your relationships is enthusiasm, which helps other people develop to their greatest potential. Yet, most of us have experienced naysayers in our lives—those people who pointed out every possible way that our dreams would not work. Those people tried to bring us down and succeeded when our resolve wasn't strong enough, plummeting us to the bottom of our doubts.

Your job is to be the yaysayer, the one who sees the possibilities in your friends' dreams, the one who projects "You can" rather than "You can't." You are not the spoiler, determining limits to someone else's ability. You do not have to set your friends straight, define what goals they can attain, or save them from failure. You share your deepest convictions with your friends that all things are possible.

Your agenda in relationships is to encourage other people to establish their personal beliefs and then to help them visualize beyond their self-limiting concepts.

My father was born right after the Great Depression. He grew up in a tiny house with one bedroom that all five children shared. He picked cotton by hand and had no spare change. He matured into someone who avoided financial risks. Even as he became increasingly successful, becoming the first child in his family to get a college degree and then a PhD, he saved each penny as if that coin would purchase his last meal. He pressed his conservative views on us. His message was to save, take no risks, and prepare for a worst case scenario. He wanted to spare us from the pain of growing up as he had—from the pain of failure. He went further and defined what he thought we could and could not do. His message to us was: Do only what he thought we could do and no more.

His intentions, however honorable they were from his perspective, were limitations. Despite his best intentions for his children, he became a naysayer, instilling in us a fear of risks and having us believe in the limits he set. It took me thirty years to overcome these beliefs, to take financial risks and to embrace my own success.

Who are you to decide what someone else cannot do? How often have people surprised you by transforming and expanding their lives in ways you had not imagined or thought possible? How often have you been mistaken when you limited your definition of someone else?

NURTURE IN OTHERS WHAT YOU BELIEVE

While enthusiasm adds great value to the relationship, being a cheerleader is not enough. Cheerleading by nature is confined to the sidelines. Cheerleaders yell their rah-rahs and then join the spectators. They get the fans excited, and the fans in turn rally the team. They are entertaining and they are part of the game, but they are not *in* the game.

As a player and as a coach, I barely noticed the cheerleaders. They were visible from the bench but were not a factor in to our wins or losses. They were not as much invested in the game as they were in their performance for the fans.

You want to be invested in your relationships with others. Being invested does not mean that you can affect the outcome of the game—whether people win or lose is up to them—but you show your support by believing in them. This belief, this show of faith, can be enough to help them remember who they really are.

In the 2006 basketball season, I had a 6'2" player, Mandy, who hated playing where she should be playing—in the paint posting up close to the basket. She wanted to shoot the 3-point shot. By mid-season, she was shooting a paltry 18% from the 3-point line, which is far below the 33% average. We were about to play the Glenville State College Pioneers at their gym to determine who was going to be number one in the conference. The Pioneers hadn't lost a game all season. I had a choice to make. I could tell Mandy to stop shooting the 3, or I could convince her to make those shots.

The practice before we played Glenville, Mandy passed up a wide open 3 point shot. I yelled, "Mandy, you shoot that shot. That's your shot. You're a great 3-point shooter. Don't think about it. Shoot it."

Trust that I was nervous saying those words. By encouraging her to shoot, I could be unleashing Pandora's Box. Giving Mandy the green light might mean that she would shoot even when should pass the ball.

During the first ten minutes of the game at Glenville State, we were down 13 points. Their crowd was in pandemonium, screaming so loudly my players couldn't hear me in the huddle. The Glenville State Pioneers were having their way with us until Mandy hit three 3 pointers in a two minute time stretch. All of a sudden, we were back in the game; and by halftime, we led by one. The crowd's enthusiasm deflated, and the momentum swung to our favor. We went on to hand the Pioneers their only three losses in a 30-win season, and Mandy was a major factor in all of those victories.

ALWAYS SHOW UP FOR THEIR BIG GAMES

When a team makes it to the play-offs, they want to see their supporters in the stands. Can you imagine a Super Bowl without the stadium being packed or a Final Four without fans displaying the color of their teams?

When people have made it to the brink of the big dance, to the moment where they could possibly win it all, they want to share the moment with the people who supported them.

It doesn't matter if the "Big Game" is an award, wedding or the first time your child has a tee-ball game. What matters is your presence. Your presence solidifies how much you care in the mind of your spouse, children, employees and friends.

All the high-fiving, fist pumping, and cheering doesn't matter if you miss the big moment. If you can't make it physically, be there by sending an email, a flower arrangement or a singing telegram. They want you to share in their success.

Every basketball season we celebrated senior night to honor our players. I considered ending this practice the year a senior was devastated when her parents failed to show up for the game. Rather than focusing on the game, her eyes constantly scanned the stands for her parents. Even though her parents did not make a regular practice of attending games, she was hopeful this one special time they would watch her play.

This was a critical game, a must win for us in order to capture the conference title. The young lady was a starter and an important member of our team. The more she focused on the stands, the worst she played on the court. During a time out I looked at her eyes and noticed tears hanging on the edge of her eyelids. Because she couldn't get her mind on the game, her passes were errant and her shots were off center. I ended up benching her for most of the second half. We barely won the contest on a last second shot.

After the game I consoled her, "I am sorry that your parents didn't come."

She wiped a tear off her cheek, "I wanted them to see how much I've improved. Why couldn't they take a few hours to watch me?"

I didn't have an answer for her question. Instead I answered, "You are amazing. You've grown so much as player and as a person. I'm proud of you who've become."

She said, "Thank you coach. I wish my parents could tell me the same thing."

My heart caught in my throat. I tried to say something else but words failed me. All this young woman wanted was to be appreciated by her parents, to be seen, and to be valued for a few hours on a Saturday night.

It doesn't matter how old we get or how much we accomplish, the moment is always better when it is shared with those we love.

We have a universal longing to be intimately known, and to be loved for who we are and what we do.

NURTURE THEIR NEEDS, NOT THEIR WANTS

In 1984, our assistant coach for the U.S. National Team Handball Team was Ilya, a native born Russian. Ilya spoke very few words of English, yet in his broken English he attempted to teach us valuable lessons. One day after he watched an episode of *Family Feud* on television, he said, "Vhat is vrong with you Americans? Vhy you clap vhen you say bad answers? On TV show, the man asked, 'Vhat color is rainbow?' The other man say, 'Black,' and everybody clapped. Vhy? This is vrong answer."

Ilya was right. It was a terrible answer. The family members should have withheld their applause. When we encourage the wrong answers, we fail both ourselves and others. We help them choose the wrong path. Our struggle is balancing the line between interference and guidance. Our job is not to rescue but to guide others into awareness through questions which trigger introspection.

When our loved ones drive too fast on a road covered with black ice, do we encourage them to drive faster? When they stand too close to the edge of a cliff, do we tell them to back up? When they are drink themselves into oblivion, do we offer them another drink? These are times when we tell them what they need to hear, not what they want to hear.

You provide integrity in your relationships through honest conversations. You assume the risk that the person with whom you share the conversation might not be ready to receive it. She might react in anger or silence, but that is not an excuse for you to duck the responsibility of having the conversation.

Susan Scott, *author of Fierce Conversations: Achieving Success at Work & in Life, One Conversation at a Time,* states "As a leader, you get what you tolerate. People do not repeat behavior unless it is rewarded. The same goes for families, our marriages, our friendships."

Due to the confidentiality of this story, the characters are renamed. Savannah was a problem drinker on one of my teams who drank even when she understood the consequences might deter her from playing the sport she loved. Her roommate, Renatta, a 20 year old, exhibited the emotional maturity of a far older and wiser individual. Most of Savannah's teammates covered for her drinking and promoted it by partying with Savannah. They rescued her from one situation after another and wanted her on the team so badly, they wouldn't dare risk telling Savannah the truth about her drinking.

Renatta, on the other hand, stood firm in her integrity about the situation. She told Savannah, "I can't room with you any longer. I worry about when or if you will make it home. I don't agree with your drinking. You are hurting yourself, and I can't bear to watch it. I love you so much I have to move out of this room."

This was a challenging journey for all of us, but Renatta stayed true to her conviction. She confronted Savannah, showed her disapproval, and never partied with her. When I presented a zero tolerance policy to Savannah, giving her the choice of drinking or playing, Renatta fully supported my decision. The other players sympathized with Savannah and criticized me. Throughout the year as Savannah struggled to remain sober, she chose Renatta as her confidant and supporter. Their relationship remained strong for years after their collegiate careers ended.

It is our duty to carry integrity through our relationships without rendering judgment. We challenge people's behaviors without having to win the conversation. We offer them the opportunity to interrogate and chose their actions. We stay true to the integrity in our offer, and surrender to the awareness it is their responsibility to reject or accept our offer.

THE EGO VERSUS THE RELATIONSHIP

FEEDING YOUR EGO

We learned from our families, coworkers, and friends how the ego needs to be massaged in relationships. The ego is the part of us that demands attention. It is constantly attempting to control others through shyness, bullying, sarcasm, cynicism, and superiority. At the core of the ego is insecurity and unworthiness.

To feed the ego we need people to say "Yes" to us, so we surround ourselves with people-pleasers, those who negate themselves so we can feel good. This relationship is based on insecurity. One person denies herself the right to be heard, and the other person denies herself the ability to speak.

When we need something from others, we give up our control to them. We might believe we are in control, but when we operate from need, we are weak. Because we haven't learned to believe in our own abilities, we depend on others to provide us with a sense of wellbeing.

This does not nurture the relationship; it abuses the relationship.

When I was a young basketball coach, I wanted to be perceived as intelligent and all-knowing. To receive respect from my players and assistant coaches, I believed they needed to hear my words of wisdom and advice. I was wise; therefore, they needed to nod their heads in agreement with my words. Their acquiescence made me feel better about myself. Consequently, they learned to withhold much needed information—information which could have made me a better basketball coach. I negated their opportunity to be valued and my opportunity to learn.

I fed my ego while denying growth opportunities. As I grew in self confidence, I learned to treasure the words of my staff and players and asked their opinions at crucial moments in the game. My assistants gained the confidence to feed me information even if that information was contradictory to my game plan. One assistant, Lynne, became crucial to the team's success; because she told me the words I needed but not necessarily wanted to hear.

We were playing in the semi-finals of the East Regional Championship Game as the number one seed in the tournament. If we won, we were in the Sweet Sixteen. If we lost, our seniors had played in their last collegiate game. We were behind by 4-6 points most of the game. When our All-American fouled out on a questionable call, I regressed to the immature Coach Winn—screaming at the officials for their incompetency. Standing noseto-nose with an official, I was on my way to a second technical foul and being ejected from the game when Lynne came up and whispered, "This is not about your ego."

The words were simple, direct and needed. I turned, headed back to the bench and coached my players. We won the game.

I learned the importance of putting my ego to rest and listening to players when the game was on the line. I asked, "What play do you want to run?" or "Who wants the ball for the last shot?" Because I asked questions and listened, the team won more games.

Anytime you try to fix somebody else, react poorly to words, take things too personally, or have the need to be in control, you feed your ego and neglect other people's possibility for personal development. You chose a lose-lose scenario denying yourself and the other person the ability to grow.

THE RELATIONSHIP ISN'T ALL ABOUT YOU

Relationships are built on mutual admiration. Both parties have something to provide and to receive. The real challenge is to remember that relationships are mutual. They are not exclusive to what you can give or receive.

In order for the relationship to evolve, you furnish something of value. Maybe that value is as down-to-earth as laughter, or maybe it is as complicated as finances in a business relationship. When you give value to others, they are dictated by social nature to reciprocate.

Robert B. Cialdini, in his book, *Influence: The Psychology of Persuasion*, states "Most of us find it highly disagreeable to be in a state of obligation. It weighs heavily on us and demands to be removed." In our social system, we have a history of reciprocal arrangements. Our early ancestors survived by bartering for food, clothes and housing. They understood when they received, they had to give back in order to keep the social system working properly. The need to reciprocate is inherent within us.

Our relationships feel out of balance without reciprocal actions. When a person offers a gift, he expects you to receive the gift and in the future, he expects you to return his favor. The gift may be kind words, a helpful action, or a physical offering. The emphasis is on the return of the gift, not on the value or cost of the gift.

I learned as a coach I could demand extreme effort from my athletes. I could push them harder than they believed they could go, and then I could push some more as long as I gave them something in return. If I failed to offer encouragement, faith, or victories, they quit on me. It couldn't just be about me and my desire to win. The training and the results had to be about them.

CELEBRATE YOUR SUCCESSES WITH OTHERS

CELEBRATION IS AN ACT OF NURTURING

Why should you take time to celebrate, to blow up balloons, to toot cardboard and plastic horns, to stream crepe paper across the walls, and to dance with your friends, family or team members? Because celebrations allow people to proclaim respect and gratitude, renew their sense of togetherness, and reinforce shared traditions.

Too often we neglect celebration. We automatically move on to the next event, the mountain in the distance or the steps on the financial ladder. What happens when we do not stop to share the elation of our accomplishments?

We isolate ourselves and close off our loved ones.

I watched the NCAA I National Championship Football game in 2012. After the game, a reporter interviewed Nick Saban, head coach of the University of Alabama and the coach of the winning team. When the reporter asked Coach Saban what he was going to do next, Coach Saban replied that he would celebrate for a couple of days and then resume working. There was no time for additional celebration, because he needed to establish the right work ethic and winning mentality for his 2013 football team.

Coach Saban's mentality represented what we have learned— *that what we accomplish is never enough.* We cannot settle for the moment or linger too long in the fun, because the consequences of getting behind our competitors are too great. If we rest or laugh, the next person will pass us by.

We must be ever diligent in our push to succeed.

I understand that mentality. I was one of those people. When I was a high school athlete, I dreamed of being an Olympian. Nobody was going to get in my way. I had tunnel vision. I had a goal. I couldn't stop to enjoy a social evening. While friends were watching movies, playing board games or toilet papering the coach's house, I was in the gymnasium. Fear drove me to practice. If I wasn't practicing to be the best, then somebody else would beat me.

I pushed until I succeeded and then I pushed some more. Like Nick Saban, I didn't allow myself much of an opportunity to celebrate. If I had decided to celebrate, I wouldn't have had any friends at the celebration. My friends disappeared when I wasn't available to join them for social activities. Too late I realized what I really wanted was the celebration with friends and family, not the trophy.

Maybe Nick Saban was smarter than me. Maybe he led a balanced life where he enjoyed family and friends and celebrated more than his interview revealed.

When you live for the next huge accomplishment and bypass the opportunity to share your triumphs, you miss the point. What good is winning or receiving rewards if you don't stop to feel the moment? Don't get me wrong. I am not opposed to monetary rewards, trophies, or achievements. We all deserve abundance.

Sometimes in our rush to achieve we forget to feel the pleasure, and by denying ourselves the pleasure, we also deny those who love us the celebration.

NURTURE YOUR BUSINESS RELATIONSHIPS

CONNECTIONS ARE ESSENTIAL

My mother thought her children should not stoop to office politics. Office politics equated to brown-nosing or kissing butt. We should earn our position, respect from others and our salaries. Consequently, I avoided networking and missed opportunities for advancement.

An old adage states, "It is not what you know; it is who you know that counts." This is true. People help people they know. The true power of attending an Ivy League University is not in the superior education, but in the networking of colleagues. When you know people who are in positions of influence, you receive additional opportunities. You still need the talent and skills to perform the job, but if you don't get inside the doors to be interviewed, those talents are worthless.

Once I got off my high horse of believing I was better than other people by getting jobs based solely on my skill, I advanced faster. My belief about the unethical nature of brown nosing held me back. I denied myself and other people the opportunity to receive my skills due to my confusion about the purpose of networking.

Networking is not kissing butt; networking connects you with other people so they can benefit from your services and you can benefit from their services. You build effective relationships through networking and unless you live in a bubble, you need relationships to function.

One of my assistant coaches, Lynne was an amazing networker. She would disappear from the office for 40-60 minutes to go across campus to chitchat with custodians, professors, administrators and facility operators. I thought this was a waste of time and almost told her so on many occasions. There was recruiting, scouting and a myriad of other tasks which needed to be done. Luckily I held my tongue. It wasn't long until I understood the value of her chitchats.

Whenever we needed the service of our custodians, they dropped whatever they were doing for somebody else and ran to help us. When our locker room needed new carpet, we were pushed to the front of assignments. When our peers were complaining about how long it took to get their computers serviced, the technicians were in our office working on our computers.

Lynne's friendliness resulted in many positive outcomes for us.

Relationships are easily built when you make everybody your friend. Lynne was a master at accepting people as they were, leaving her judgment out of the picture. When her acquaintances had different politics, religions or viewpoints about the economy, she allowed them to have their beliefs, keeping her opinions to herself.

Lynne's networking was more than creating business relationships. Through her connections, she also had the ability to serve more people. The more people she connected with, the more opportunities emerged for her and the team to help others. This is the value of connections. You take the time to know others and to let them know you to discover how the relationship can become mutually beneficial.

NETWORKING ALLOWS NURTURING

To get people to associate with you, look for ways to help them advance. Many people fear if they help somebody else advance that person will leapfrog over them to gain the advantage. The belief that all people are worthy of abundance and there is limitless abundance quashes your fears. By believing that abundance abounds, you are free to give assistance to others.

W. Clement Stone said, "Your most precious, valued possessions and your greatest powers are invisible and intangible. No one can take them. You and you alone, can give them. You will receive abundance for your giving."

When you help other people profit, progress or gain power, you help yourself. You are limited by the belief that what you give is gone. When you give from the center of abundance, you recognize your life is overflowing and that by giving, you remain full.

If you struggle with the principle of abundance, take a moment to reflect on how much money the rich give away. In 2012, both Warren Buffet and The Bill and Melinda Gates Foundation gave away 2 billion dollars. Buffet has pledged that his 58 billion dollars will all be given away before or after his death. Chuck Feeney has given away 7.5 billion and is still pledging more money to various organizations. Oprah Winfrey and Ellen DeGeneres are legendary for giving away money to their audience members and people in need. Oprah donates approximately 25 million a year while Ellen gets people to help her raise and donate over 30 million dollars a year.

You might believe people give money away because they have the money, but maybe they have the money because they shared their riches. Abundance cannot come to you if refuse to share.

When you resist from others what you desire, you also resist it from yourself.

> "Never forget, then, that you set the value on what you receive, and price it by what you give…The recognition of having is the willingness for giving, and only by this willingness can you recognize what you have."
> — A Course in Miracles

NURTURE RELATIONSHIPS THROUGH MARKETING

My friend, James Malinchak, the Big Money Speaker says, "You should Always Be Marketing." How do people know what you can do if you don't tell them? Do you think people will recognize your brilliance? Perhaps…but that is taking a chance on hitting the lottery. You might be one of the lucky ones, but why wait for the unlikely when you can promote your brilliance today?

If you believe your abilities can help other people and you are not sharing those abilities, then you are selfish. You waste your talents by not sharing them with those in need. You cannot nurture others when you are hidden from their view.

I thought if I coached my players to win games, people would recognize my greatness. Our fans acknowledged my coaching ability, and my players also applauded my coaching skills. Neither of these two groups of people were influential in helping me get another job.

The only way I got jobs was through marketing myself. Unfortunately, I didn't toot my own horn enough. I was swindled by the belief promoting myself was dishonest. I waited to receive the lottery rather than marketing my talents.

People don't recognize our brilliance when we hide it from them. We nurture relationships by telling people matter-of-factly what we can do. When you are confident in yourself, you talk about your talents in a true-life, down-to-earth manner. People accept your strengths and accomplishments as long as you don't appear brash or arrogant.

You've probably met people who turned you off, because they dropped names as if those associations made them more important. They talked about all the things they accomplished, their awards and recognitions until you wanted to puke. They turned you off because they were trying too hard to make an impression.

What is the difference between showing off and marketing yourself? When you try to impress others, you push your accomplishments on them. When you market, you tell people what you've done in terms of how that can help them. Your desire is to nurture the relationship. You are focused on them, not you.

Any good speaker knows the key to capturing an audience—the WIIFM factor. They make certain to think like the audience who is wondering WHAT'S IN IT FOR ME? This is how people think. People want to know how they will profit from knowing or hiring you. When you give them useful information that is sensible and practical, they will want to do business with you.

For 20 years I didn't tell people I was a two-time Olympian. I didn't want to flaunt my talents. I didn't want people to talk about how I thought I was important. The problem wasn't the other people; it was me. I felt uncomfortable talking about my successes, because I didn't believe in my self-worth. By keeping my talents to myself, I withheld my ability to nurture others.

Once I understood how valuable I truly was, then I was able to share my successes with others. This was not a cocky factor; it was an awareness factor. I had something valuable to share with others. Because I finally understood I was worthy, I could talk about myself without needing to impress others.

People who talk incessantly about themselves and their accomplishments don't believe in themselves. They try to convince themselves they are okay by spewing out titles and acquaintances. This makes you uncomfortable because you recognize their need for acceptance. They are not prepared to nurture; they need nurturing.

When you share information, listen and value others, you can market how you can assist them without being pushy. When they take the time to know you, they will benefit from the relationship. You should always be marketing yourself, because others deserve to have what you offer.

METHODS FOR NURTURING RELATIONSHIPS

1. Become a member of Face Book. Update your status daily. Read the status of your acquaintances and friends. Comment on their status. Like their pages.

2. Whenever you meet new people, enter their email address under a special heading for networking contacts. Email them within 24 hours after the initial meeting. Every time there is a special holiday or event, drop them a few lines.

3. When people do something special for you, return the favor. Write them a personal hand-written note. Write five hand-written notes in the next five days even if the note is a thank you for something which occurred several years ago.

4. List five people who you want to create special relationships with. Write down three ways you can serve them.

5. Make a list of 25 reasons why people should want to know you and be your friend.

6. Record 10 ways your ego gets in the way of your relationships. (**The need to be right, gossiping, etc.**)

7. Write down 5 ways you prevent yourself from having great relationships with the people you need to know. Then write down a way to meet the person you want to know and what you will offer him.

8. Evaluate what you tolerate in your relationships. Make a list of five peers, friends or family members. Beside each name write down a way you allow them to behave which is not beneficial for their future.

CHAPTER SIX

EXPECT THE BEST

WE GROW AS WE SEE OURSELVES

EXPECT THE BEST

"Treat a man as he is and he will remain as he is. Treat a man as he can and should be and he will become as he can and should be."
— Stephen R. Covey

Have you lived your life to meet other people's expectations? Did you fail after your father called you a failure, or because your teacher said you would never be more than a janitor? Did you quit playing basketball because a coach told you that you couldn't shoot? Did you abandon your dream of being an adventure guide when your brother said you were too dumb to find your way out of a paper bag?

Growing up, I molded myself to the expectations of others. I became what my coaches fed me. When my Olympic coach called me stupid, I believed him despite the fact I was a 4.0 student. I played out his low expectations with stupid mistakes on the court. The more mistakes I made and the more he called me stupid, the more right he seemed, and the more my 4.0 GPA felt like the anomaly. This happened despite that fact that I wasn't young and impressionable; I was 26 years old and should have known better than to listen to someone else's opinion of me.

What happened to my performance in response to the coach's condemnation of my skills? What happened to my energy? Did I sustain maximum effort? No! Destroying my confidence meant that I lost the motivation to train.

I blamed my coach because I didn't trust my ability, on or off the court. I permitted him to judge my worth. If I had rejected his assessment, I could have performed at my highest capacity. Instead, I dropped my expectations of myself to match his.

Self-actualization involves the awareness that we take charge of what we hear and that we can choose to apply and sustain that awareness for our own benefit. When we have high expectations of others, we raise their opportunities to succeed.

In 1990 I coached the University of Minnesota-Morris Cougars, a small, private institution with no scholarships. The young women who played for me not only paid their way to go to college but trained under my grueling command. In December of that year, we played Mankato State University, a NCAA II university with 10 full ride scholarships. We lost the game by 10 points, and I was ecstatic. I viewed the loss as a victory. We didn't have the talent or the financial backing to compete with them, yet we made them play hard to earn their victory.

Later that same year we played Mankato again on their home court without one of our starters, Kris, who had suffered a mild concussion in the previous game. I knew there was no way we could defeat Mankato, but I told my players we had an ace in the hole. Kris had played a stellar game against Mankato a month ago, and I was certain their coach had been diligently training her players to defend Kris. Mankato wouldn't be prepared for what we were going to bring. We would surprise them.

I didn't believe this bunch of hogwash I fed my players. I feared that we would get our butts whipped, but I kept up the cover story. In fact, I carried the story out by having Kris wear her uniform and warming up with the team, presenting the idea she was going to play in the game. My players trusted me enough to buy the story hook, line and sinker.

And do you believe it? We beat Mankato by 10 points! The players lived up to my expectations and exceeded them. This is the power of expecting the best. You bring people up and let their ability surprise you.

You receive the same thing from yourself through high expectations. When you give your best and expect to be your best, you most often are.

UTILIZE 2M THINKING

What is 2M thinking? 2M thinking is the ability to maximize or minimize your thoughts about events in your life. You can choose to think bigger or smaller. How you perceive your thoughts determines how you feel and react. In turn, your reaction brings into being your success or failure.

I struggled in my early years believing I had no control over what happened to me. I saw life through a victim's eyes, believing that life controlled me. I was on earth for the ride and was trying to survive the bumps.

Oh, I heard some of the platitudes preached:

- "The only person who is ever right is the person who says "I can't.""
- "In order to achieve, you must first believe."
- "Focus on the things that you can do, not the things you cannot do."

These were just quotes my coaches threw out at practices. I had no sense of their depth or the meaning behind the words.

The idea of controlling my thoughts first came when I was playing basketball at Texas A&M University. A graduate student administered a survey to the team. The survey questions pertained to the player's reactions to officials, our teammates, the fans and the coaches.

My answers to that survey reflected a profound sense that I lacked control. At that time a little sliver of awakening bubbled up in my awareness. I felt the nudge but didn't have the power to focus on the question. I wasn't ready to wake up.

It wasn't until I hung up my shoes as an athlete and started to coach that I noticed how much my players' attitudes affected their behavior. When my players focused on a poor call by the officials and ramped up their protest, they maximized their emotions and forgot how to play basketball. Maximizing anger at a teammate for not quickly passing the ball to them created a mistake in their next offensive assignment. Getting mad at me for yelling at them put their focus on me instead of the game.

I pilfered away some of my athletic talent by maximizing negative thoughts and minimizing positive thoughts. To help my players avoid suffering the same consequence, I researched methods to help them. The first concept to catch my eye was recognizing the difference between uncontrollable and controllable factors.

Uncontrollable factors are people, situations, and events. For athletes, these things might include the temperature of the gym, the number of fans in the stands, the opponents' style of play, injuries or illnesses, the way the officials called the game, the condition of the floor, their teammates, and of course, the coaching staff. Controllable factors included variables like attitudes, reactions, emotions, effort, work ethic, hustle, determination, heart, confidence, personal skill, and communication. Controllable factors could change the way players felt about uncontrollable factors.

If I controlled my reactions to events by maximizing positive thoughts and minimizing negative thoughts, it was almost as good as controlling the event. If an official made a bad call with ten seconds left to go in the game—giving our opponents a one-in-one free throw attempt and the opportunity to get the go-ahead basket—and I freaked out at the official, we were probably going to lose. My players would follow my lead, freak out, and act as if we had already lost.

But, wait. Even if the free throws were made, ten seconds still remained in the game. Most players could run down the court and back in ten seconds.

The game was not over in **real time**; *it was just over in our minds.*

If we concentrated on what we could control and maximized our thoughts toward winning, our focus turned to scoring the winning basket. When we believed we were going to win, no matter what happened in the game, we found a way to win.

Sports are made from momentum and that momentum is shifted throughout the game by great plays and reactions to those plays. If one of my players threw the ball away and reacted by having a temper tantrum or quitting, rather than by hustling back to play defense, my player gave her opponents not only the ball and a basket, but an unearned boost of energy.

If after my player threw the ball away, she had minimized the mistake in her head and hustled back to play defense, the opponent got only the ball and maybe a basket but no momentum. The difference is crucial to the play. Minimizing her negative reaction to the play prevented the opponents from thinking that they got the upper hand. This was the key to winning—minimizing or maximizing our reactions to events so we could hang on to the game's momentum.

This is also the key to winning your game. Isn't life exactly like a game? There are some events like falling in love where you gain momentum, and other events like being demoted in a job where you lose momentum. Your constant is the ability to master your reactions so you determine how they feel to you, choosing to focus on success no matter what events occur.

Before I taught my athletes the value of 2M thinking, most of them failed to connect their reactions to the outcome of a game. Have you discovered how your thinking dictates your reactions which determine your outcomes? By changing your thoughts, you will be surprised at how events in your life change.

EMPOWERMENT BEGINS WITH TUNING IN TO THE RIGHT STATION

If I had known about 2M thinking as a teenager or young adult, I would not have followed the victim's path and would have found happiness earlier in my life. Understanding how influential my thoughts were and learning the extent to which I could control them was empowering.

Why do we not succeed at a goal? Because we fail to empower ourselves.

**Empowerment is recognizing that the force
to create opportunities dwells within us.
IT IS US.**

Doesn't it feel wonderful to know that you can create what you desire? After all those years of blaming and feeling inadequate, thinking you had to wait for the perfect opportunity to get what you wanted, doesn't it feel good to know that you hold the power to determine your own reality?

Derek Rydall, a motivational leader, says, "Wherever you are, your favorite music is playing, but you can't hear it until you tune into the right station."

Maybe what has been happening to you is that you have been listening to all the wrong stations, unaware that you had to reach inside yourself to turn the dial. You can train yourself to turn the dial to awareness and alternative ways of thinking like dialing into 2M thinking.

What a great place to begin. You can change your outlook on life in a day. You can find peace in any setting. By looking, you can find the good in every situation, event and person.

A SLIGHT CHANGE IN FOCUS CREATES DREAMS

Kristen was 6'3" and a tough competitor. She was a member of the Northern Montana Skylights, a team which averaged 88 points per game and beat opponents by a 20 point margin. On the '93 Skylight team, there were eight players who were capable of scoring double digits, and eight players who were not satisfied with their scoring; they all wanted to be the star.

Kristen was one of those players who thought she should get the ball more during our offensive possessions, so she came to my office to present her case.

> **Kristen:** "Coach, I think I should be getting the ball more on offense. You know I'm a good shooter, and my shooting percentage is really high."

> **Me:** "You are good shooter, and I'm glad you think you should be scoring more points. Every player should always be looking for ways to become better. So what are you going to do about it?"

> **Kristen:** "What do you mean what **AM I** going to do about it? I'm in here talking to you."

> **Me:** "I want you to focus on maximizing what you can control and minimizing what you can't control. What are the things that you can maximize?"

> **Kristen:** "Well . . . I can crash the offensive boards harder and get more opportunities for second chance baskets."

> **Me:** "Awesome. Yes, you can create more points that way."

> **Kristen:** "I can run harder on fast breaks. I know I can get a couple more baskets that way."

> **Me:** "Great."

> **Kristen:** "I can seal my defender better and call for the ball. You know how the guards never see the posts, so I'll let them know I'm open."

Me: "That is awesome Kristen. You've just found three different ways to score more baskets."

As she was opening the door to leave my office, she turned and with a mischievous smile said, "And I'm going to make dang sure the point guard is my best friend!"

The point guard is the player who is responsible for calling the plays and getting the ball in the hands of our scorers. Kristen maximized her time with our point guard, Jodi, by sitting next to her at meals, protecting her on the court, and complimenting her on her tremendous passes.

Kristen went on to become an All-American player that season and helped us to a 35-3 record and the first ever national championship at Northern Montana College. The coaching staff never altered our offensive scheme, nor did we create special plays for Kristen. She created her opportunities to score by focusing on maximizing the events she could control, and by making certain the point guard was her best friend.

HOW TO FEEL GOOD AND GET WHAT YOU DESIRE

THE LAW OF ATTRACTION

If you are familiar with the premise of the Law of Attraction, you know the following: *Like attracts like; you get what you think about most of the time; or it is done to you as you believe.* Your expectations become your reality, which is why you must expect the best. By controlling your thoughts and keeping them tuned into what you desire, you create the life that you want. By focusing on negative possibilities, though, you can also create what you don't want.

One of the most critical elements for utilizing the Law of Attraction is to **FEEL GOOD**, to arrive at the belief that your positive expectations have already happened. How can you do this when you have lost a loved one, when your body is sick, when you have been fired from a job, or when the partner you loved has betrayed you?

How can you get into this feel-good place when the reality all around you is not the reality that you desire?

You realize that you *cannot know the meaning of an event.* You have no power to see beyond the moment. What you believe to be horrific may open the doorway to your dreams. You cannot know what you do not know.

I dreamed of being an Olympian since the age of seven. But my freshmen year at the University of Houston was a disaster. I mostly sat on the bench, something I had never done in my athletic career. In high school softball, basketball and volleyball, I was the star. By the time I was a sophomore in college, my dream was fast disappearing. Life was not going well for me. I had gained 20 pounds, drank beer like it was air, and was slipping in and out of depression.

I transferred to Texas A&M, trained all summer long, lost the 20 pounds and came back my sophomore year ready to play ball. I was the leading scorer on the team, but not a player coveted by my teammates. The season ended in a blur with me quitting the team after a volatile team meeting with my teammates. I felt mortally wounded by their venomous words. I nosedived into depression and used alcohol as medication. Life seemed finished.

A month later because I wasn't playing basketball, a classmate introduced me to the sport of team handball. This introduction opened the door for me to play on the national team handball team and compete in the World Championships, the Pan American Games, the Goodwill Games, and the 1984 and 1988 Olympic Games.

The dream I sought could not have been delivered to me until I gave up basketball. As long as I played basketball, I wasn't available to try out other sports. Instead of crushing my dreams, my basketball teammates helped create an opening for my dream to be delivered to me.

When I was depressed and separate from my Olympic dream, I lived what I felt and saw with my physical eyes and being. I had no faith in an inner vision because I lost the alignment with my dream. I believed that I was talented enough to be an Olympian, but I didn't believe in my worthiness to be one.

What sounds so simple is complex, because we exist in a visual state. We do not see what we manifest through our requests, because our requests are not evidenced in physical reality. We lack faith that what we ask for is already created. Instead of moving forward and acting as if we already have our desires, we stay in a continual state of living what we see.

When you become impatient and ask, "Where is what I requested?" you go directly to feeling the lack of not having your desires. When you don't have what you want, you feel anxious, bitter, worried, frustrated, discouraged, dejected, and allow hopelessness to creep into your heart and brain. You become the opposite of the very thing you desire.

The key is to keep the faith, to believe in your dreams, to act as if they are coming to you no matter what your eyes tell you, and to continue moving forward toward what you desire. Feeling good is necessary to attracting your dreams. When you feel you are pushing against your goals, you are not aligned. When you are frustrated or impatient, you are not where you need to be. Expect what you want, believe you will get it, and surrender the struggle.

WE CANNOT CONTRADICT THAT WHICH WE ARE

In November 2013 some parents from Montana disowned their daughter because she came out as a lesbian. The parents' religious origins taught that homosexuality was a sin, and they chose not to love the "sin" of their daughter. They also decided that they couldn't love their daughter.

This story is not about determining who is right or wrong but about the choices of love and of judgment.

Why is this lesson important to you?

When you hold an absence of love within, you harbor negative vibrations. You block the greatest source of energy from flowing through you. Positive vibrations attract more of the things you love. You cannot expect the best for yourself and yet hold negative energy at the same time. Positive and negative energy cancel each other out.

We can easily love some people and hate others, believing in an invisible line that we can draw between love and hate, an invisible barrier that immunizes us from the negative vibrations of hate. We should hate those who are bad. Right?

A quote from *A Course in Miracles* states:

"When you meet anyone, remember it is a holy encounter. As you see in him, you will also see in yourself. As you treat him, you will also treat yourself.

You cannot separate your emotion from the emotion you feel for others. If you harbor hostility, disgust, or hatred in your judgment of others, that negativity does not just jump on them and leave you. The residue of emotion remains. What you think you are giving away to another is, in fact, what you offer yourself.

If you want to attract love but also to withhold love, you offer at once both a positive and a negative vibration. You negate yourself by pulling in opposite directions.

Ask yourself, "Which side do I want to win?" The side which withholds love from another because I do not understand or agree with her, or the side of me which believes I am worthy of unconditional love even though I cannot give it?

Maybe you judged the parents who disowned their daughter for honoring their religious beliefs. Or maybe you judged the daughter who is a lesbian. The question is: How does that judgment feel within you? Judgment determines your ability to attract. The more negative vibrations within you, the less you will attract what you desire. To expect and receive the best life has to offer, maintain a high level of positive emotions.

How do you learn to be more loving and nonjudgmental?

This is a lifelong quest, but you can begin with simple steps:

1. Become more aware of how your expressed emotions feel inside you.
2. Say "I love you" to yourself, over and over.
3. Practice the art of empathy.
4. Recognize harmful judgments and release them.
5. Align yourself with people on a quest of personal development.

By learning to love more and judge less, you will align yourself with greater opportunity.

THE "YES, BUTS" AND TAIL-ENDERS OF KILLING YOUR DREAMS

The premise of getting what you want is simple: you receive what you expect to receive most of the time. If you are conscious of your desires and keep that desire uppermost in your mind, you will receive it.

The core concept is basic; once learned it can manifest all your aspirations.

The problem is that we first must learn to control all of our thoughts, because every thought is creative. One thought does not possess more power than another, until we put the power of our absolute conviction behind it.

In other words, most of us want something we don't think we can have, or we want something but don't see how to get it. Our doubt interferes with the conviction underlying the thought, as evidenced when we express our doubt in "Yes, but" statements.

- "Yes, I want a new job *but* I don't see how that can happen right now."

- "Yes, I would love to have a partner who supports me, *but* I've never had that in the past."

- "Yes, I want to get rid of chronic pain, *but* I've had it for so long that I don't think it will ever go away."

We say what we want but in the same breath negate the conviction. We cannot truly feel what we desire. We hope and want, but we don't **believe**. Faith is essential to create what we want in our life.

Another way to devalue our goals is to use tail-enders in sentences. Tail-enders are phrases that come after "but" and "because" to rationalize why we can't have, be or do something. Tail-enders defend our lack of belief in having what we desire.

- I never became the writer I wanted to be, *because* my 4th grade teacher told me that I was not smart enough to write correctly.

- I was going to start my own company *but* never did, *because* my father told me there is no security in self-employment.

- I would have been the CEO of that company, *but* I never got the opportunity *because* I'm not social enough to be on the board of trustees.

Most of us are great at dreaming while believing we do not deserve our dreams to come true. We empower our doubts while neglecting to strengthen our faith. We imagine all sorts of impediments to our desires through wishy-washy thoughts.

Every thought has power.

While we can't control each and every thought that enters our awareness, we can learn to listen for the conviction or doubt behind the words we speak. Learning to emphasize positive emotions with our thoughts will help minimize our doubts. Learning to think positively with conviction will put us on the path to manifesting our desires.

DOES REQUESTING YOUR DESIRES CREATE NEGATIVE VIBRATION?

What is the perfect number of times to request your desires?

How many times must you ask before expecting to receive?

We can get stuck in the asking mode. After all, we do that all our lives. When young, we asked our mother or father for something over and over, hoping they would relent. We bugged a brother or sister to ride in their car until we heard, "Okay." As a sidelined athlete, we pestered the coach for a chance to play on the court.

We learned that asking over and over would most of the time result in getting what we wanted.

So if we ask the Universe over and over again to get what we desire, does that contradict the power to expect the best in our lives? One would think that asking for our goals to be met over and over again would be good. The more determinedly we ask and demand a response, the more the Universe should reward us by meeting our desires.

The problem with multiple asking is that you are in danger of begging. Your parents might have given in to your demands as a child, because you wore them down to exhaustion, but the Universe doesn't work that way.

When you continually ask, are you asking from a sense of having (fulfillment) or from a sense of wanting (loss)? What is your energy and how do you feel when you beg for something? What vibration is whining? The more you ask, the more you focus on what you do not have. This desperation directly opposes your ability to expect the best.

When asking becomes begging, are you aligned with expecting the best in your life? You cannot, because when you ask while focusing on what you lack, you cannot also sustain already fulfilled desire. The concept behind the Law of Attraction is that you get what you think about most of the time.

How then do you continue to think about what you desire without asking?

1. Develop a daily habit to visualize in detail what you ask for from the Universe. Add color, sound, texture and emotion. The more real you can make your visualization experience, the closer you are to bringing it to life.

2. Devote a time each day imagining that you already have what you want. If you want a new house, go visit new houses. Look at them; pretend you own the home. Picture yourself hosting a dinner party in your new home. Watch your children running around the house and enjoy the view. Make the house yours in your own mind.

3. Go to the store or online and imagine purchasing items that you want. Spend your mental money on them and enjoy the splurge, without spending real dollars.

4. Make a vision board. Find pictures and representations of goals, objects and desires for your life, and make them into a collage. You may be surprised at how your subconscious mind reveals itself and its desires through play.

During your imagining, stop immediately if you find yourself blocked by thoughts that you can't have or that you don't deserve what you want. Trying to figure out the details is another trap to avoid, because you might get lost in believing that your goal is too hard or impossible. Remember that the most important aspect of a daydreaming game is to have fun. Enjoyment is everything in this type of play.

A helpful method with an imagination exercise is to start small. Begin with desires that you believe you can and deserve to have. If you begin by asking for a million dollars when you currently earn $50,000, your mind will likely not be ready for the leap. Start small and build confidence as you succeed with the process.

Ask once and then believe.

The outcome is created not by the asking, but by the faith.

THE LAW OF ACTION

One aspect of expecting the best or the Law of Attraction that many people avoid is ACTION. By working on your mind you believe what you want to achieve, but belief alone is not sufficient. You must take action after cultivating the ideas and dreams in your mind.

The first step is intention, knowing what you want and having the intention to achieve it, but how many people have you met who intended to do a thing but never took the first step? They told you they wanted to stop smoking, lose weight or get into better shape, but their words were not followed by actions.

In 1994 my assistant coach caught one of our players, who I will call Marissa, smoking a cigarette in the bathroom before a game. Marissa and I sat down to have a conversation about our smoking policy.

"Marissa, smoking is against team policy.

Unable to look at me, Marissa put her head down before responding. "I know. I promise I will quit."

"Do you understand what's at stake here? The consequences of breaking team rules is to revoke your scholarship."

"I understand."

At the end of the season I brought Marissa back into my office for another discussion. "Marissa, it has come to my attention that you're still smoking. You and I had an agreement that you would quit."

She looked defiantly at me, "I did quit."

"When?"

"The day you told me. I quit in my mind that day; I just haven't gotten my body to follow through yet."

Marissa had focused her thoughts on the outcome she wanted, but she failed to take subsequent action. Failing to take the action steps cost Marissa her position on the team and her scholarship.

People who succeed by expecting and receiving the best in their lives devote themselves to moving toward their goals. A good way to start is to write them down. Something magical happens when you write goals down on paper. The goal seems to get a life of its own. Writing a goal down transforms it to a possibility staring back at you and asks you what action is required to complete it. The act of writing creates a permanent record, showing that you are serious, accountable, and moving through a process to reach your goal.

Writing your goals is an action step. You make a promise to yourself. The next step is to take action and move toward your goals. How do you do this?

Review the goals you've written down so far. Take one goal and break it down. What do you want to accomplish in the next 30 days? Write down what you need to do every day to reach your 30 day goal.

Then, take another action. Do this even if the action feels small and unimportant. Keep moving. Making mistakes is part of the process. You assess and reassess your actions as you move forward.

Other points to keep in mind:

1. Take responsibility for your dreams.

2. Continue to attend to your thoughts, because how you think matters.

3. Have a dream big enough to move you beyond obstacles.

4. Commit time every day to study and learn.

5. Act as if your success is certain.

6. Share your dreams.

7. Stretch your mind to visualize all possibilities.

When you train your mind to focus positively on what you want rather than negatively on what you don't want, you are expecting the best. This training supports your dream and your belief in its achievement. Expecting the best provides the faith you need to take action.

All that remains is for you to take the first step and then the next and then the next, until you are no longer just thinking about your goals but you are living them.

THE NEXT STEP

1. Take a situation from your past which didn't work out well for you. Maybe it was an argument with a partner, a situation with a co-worker at your job, or a fall-out with your supervisor. Write down how you reacted. What did you say? What did your body language tell

the other person? How did the other person react to your reaction? Write down your alternative reactions that could potentially diffuse the situation.

2. List 5 things you don't have control over.

3. List 10 things you have control over.

4. Write down 20 ways your life would improve if you chose to maximize positive reactions.

5. What is the one negative reaction that has become a habit for you? How would you feel differently if you minimized that reaction to the size of a peanut and maximized a positive reaction the size of an elephant?

WRITE DOWN YOUR GOALS USING THE ACTION METHOD

Write down three goals for each of these areas: health, finances, relationships, and spirituality.

1. A-Are **measureable** and specific. Goals are nebulous when written as hopes or wishes. Write them as action steps. *(I will run a marathon.)*

2. C-**Commit** to the completion of the goal. You need a big reason for accomplishing the goal. Write down the compelling reason you want to achieve this goal. *(REASON-I want to commit to better health by doing something I believe is impossible for me; thereby giving me confidence, muscle tone, and a slimmer body.)*

3. Time-specific. Give yourself a **time** for when the goal should be completed. Create a sense of urgency. *(I will run a marathon in 12 months from today.)*

4. Inspiring. Your goals should **inspire** you to complete them by making you feel good when you visualize

them. *(When daily visualizing yourself at the finish line, you should feel elation.)*

5. **O-Ownership** of the goal. You take total responsibility for your success and put your "Yes, but" statements to rest. Write down your beliefs which might prevent you from success, so you recognize them and can get through them. *(I would train to run a marathon but I've never run further than 5 miles. I would run every day but I can't because I've got to work. Remind yourself these are just excuses and not real reasons.)*

6. **N-Navigate** your goals by writing out smaller objectives which can be completed quicker. Celebrate these small successes as you complete them. *(I will run 3 miles for six days my first week of training. On Sunday, I will celebrate with two scoops of my favorite ice cream.)*

CHAPTER SEVEN

RECOVER FROM YOUR PAST

GETTING BEYOND YOURSELF

We prevent ourselves from having what we desire by living in our past stories. By believing our experiences determine our future outcomes; we trap ourselves into the past. Who we were is a determinant of who we become *if we allow it*. **We have the choice to learn from our past, release our past or live in our past.**

Many people assume they have moved beyond their past because they married another person, swapped jobs, or switched religious beliefs. They changed scenery but still suffer from past beliefs. They blame their husband or their boss for their failures, have excuses for why they haven't accomplished their goals, believe that suffering leads to better behaviors, judge themselves or others, or make themselves miserable by needing to be right. Thinking the same thoughts lead to the same outcomes. They are addicted to their past.

You can live in the now and create your future by changing your thoughts. You live past stories by believing in them. You cannot change the events of your past, but you can alter how you perceive them. Releasing the negative emotions attached to your past furnishes you new possibilities for the present, which in turn grants you a new future.

WHAT IS A VICTIM?

People who blame outside circumstances, events or people for their problems are victims. They live in their old excuses connecting their past to their present which explains why they cannot have what they desire. We categorize people as victims rather than seeing ourselves as victims. We hear when other people blame events or people for for their demise, but do we hear ourselves?

- "The reason I can't get ahead in life is that I never developed the right connections."

- "I can't lose the weight because my family is all overweight. It is genetics."

- "It is not about what you know; it is about who you know. I don't know the right people to get a good job."

- "I would have been a great athlete, but my father always told me that I would be a failure."

- "I would have gone into business for myself, but my high school teacher told me that 95% of all entrepreneurs fail."

Some people call these reasons but they are **excuses.** You determined not to receive your desires through your excuses. You connected your past failures to your future endeavors. I'm guilty. I've used excuses to shove the blame away from me. I've pointed my finger at somebody else claiming it was not my fault.

But does an excuse help you feel better or does it chain you to mediocrity?

Decide to stop your victim mentality and start taking responsibility for your character, circumstances, and failures. As long as you find reasons why you can't be, do or have something, you remain stuck and powerless. Accepting responsibility for your actions and outcomes leads you to pursuing and finding solutions.

Sarah understood the power of accepting responsibility. She defeated three types of cancer in her life. The last cancer she overcame was stage four lymphoma. Her physician believed her outlook was so bad he recommended she spend the next few weeks saying goodbye to family and friends. Instead, she searched for and found solutions. Sarah chose not to succumb to the victim mentality or to her doctor's past experiences with stage four lymphoma patients.

Sarah shows what is possible when you decide to take responsibility for the creation of your life. No excuses. No reasons. JUST SOLUTIONS.

MISERY IS A SIGN OF VICTIMHOOD

Did you ever hear the platitude, "Misery loves company?" Not only does misery love company. It demands it. Miserable people drag others into their misery by sharing their past stories.

The first day I arrived at college I told my roommate my STORY about how high school teammates booed me when I received the tournament MVP trophy, how they tried to vote me off the team, and how one teammate quit rather than play beside me on defense. I then told another person and another. I wanted to tell everybody my story—the story about how other people hurt and abandoned me. I repeated my poor-me story wanting to be validated. I yearned that my new friends would hate my old enemies as much as I did.

I made that story my excuse platform which solidified my victimhood. Had I been confident and secure in my abilities, I wouldn't have had the need to drive the blame elsewhere. I would have persevered through trials and errors.

I lived in unconscious incompetence. I didn't know my insecurity drove my victimhood and my victimhood thwarted my success.

I lost empowerment by continuing to say things like, "If Barbara wouldn't have been the nasty person she was and influenced the rest of the team, I would have had a better athletic career. If the officials wouldn't have hated me so much and fouled me out, I would have averaged more points. If my mother and father wouldn't have fought so much, I would have had better relationships."

I remained fixated in my past every time I told those stories and convinced myself that Barbara, the officials, or my parents determined the outcome of my life. They held all the power for me and ran my life through their control buttons.

How many times have you used an excuse for the reason you didn't get what you wanted? Did you realize what you were doing? Did you ever ask yourself why you needed somebody else to be your scapegoat?

I needed the excuses because deep down I didn't believe I could do it.

But how many people want to admit they don't believe in themselves? Isn't it easier to place the blame rather than to accept the responsibility that you control your life?

The problem with finger pointing is that when you continue to blame others, you realize you don't have the power to change them. Your powerlessness leads to frustration then exasperation, which can cause you to nosedive into desperation and eventually depression. You are miserable because you can't see an escape. You continue to live your story wondering why life never changes.

If you keep telling the same story, you get the same results. I kept telling the same story. What stories are you telling?

BEING RIGHTEOUS IS A FORM OF VICTIMHOOD

I was taught being righteous was a positive quality—one of integrity and honor. I discovered it was another form of victimhood.

Perhaps you've been taught that righteousness means to be respectable, moral, and upright. It does denote those things, and it also means blameless. Blameless by definition means unblemished, untarnished and guiltless. By being blameless, you inherently focus on NOT taking responsibility for your past actions. You separate yourself from others by judging your actions as more worthy.

Being righteous is not about morality or respectability; it is about judgment. Can you feel good about yourself without the need for comparison? If you can, congratulations. You have worked on seeing the good within you and have no need to make yourself feel better by judging others.

It took me 20 years to discover my righteousness was a form of judgment, and that judgment was another way to be a victim.

I implemented this tool of righteousness to convince myself I was worthy. I needed to feel superior because I wasn't fully invested in self love. I wasn't good enough so therefore I needed to feel better by believing somebody else was less than me. I failed to understand that by pointing our other people's sins, problems and inadequacies, I could end up hurt or lonely.

I got both.

When I was training on the national team handball team for the 1984 Olympic Games, I was known for my belligerence. It was not uncommon for me to stop during a drill and ask the coaches, "What is the purpose of this drill?" I didn't ask because I wanted to know. *I asked because I believed my coaches didn't know, and I wanted to expose their ignorance.*

I didn't question my incentives. I believed I was right, and therefore I needed to point out my coaches' blunders. Now I realize I needed validation. Other people should recognize and confirm my intelligence. They needed to do this for me, because I resided in the history of my condemnation.

My coaches were not high performance coaches, and fighting against them did not make the situation better. It didn't make me smarter or my coaches better. Eventually I became labeled an antagonist as I continued confronting their errors. The relationship became tenuous and resulted in me almost being dismissed from the team. In my victim mentality, it never dawned me I was responsible for our poor relationship. *They were the ones who were incompetent.*

Do you see how this all ties into victimhood? When you are a victim, you have the need to criticize others so you can perceive yourself as smarter, better and more capable. You gave your power to achieve away, so you feel hopeless. You can't tolerate other people having success, because you believe it is impossible for you. The only way for you to feel good is to bring other people down to your level.

Steve Maraboli, author of *Unapologetically You: Reflections on Life and the Human Experience*, reflected, "Most haters are stuck in a poisonous mental prison of jealousy and self-doubt that blinds them to their own potentiality."

Maybe you have a similar story, one where you felt like you were mistreated, and where you made yourself out to be the hero. Can you see how you made yourself the victim? Reflect on the thoughts that brought you into that process. Can you see where making yourself the hero in your tale is more about wanting somebody else to look bad, so you can look better?

LEARNING THE NO-EXCUSES RULE

I still pull out the victim card. Most of the time I am able to catch myself before going too far down the rabbit hole and tuck it away, but sometimes I ignore my intuition and use it anyway. The results are always the same. I pretend I am not responsible, wasting my breath on how the world isn't fair, and how some people are born lucky. Every time I invoke the victim card, I don't reach my goals.

If you are a victim, it is time to start taking responsibility—time to make the "no excuses" rule.

I coached a player from 2005-2009 who possessed incredible athleticism. Jihan was quick, athletic and could jump up and touch the rim, and she was also full of excuses. She had a reason for all her failures. The first three seasons she played for me, she performed below her potential. At the end of her junior year, we sat down together and had a conversation.

Me: "Jihan, How do you feel about the past three years?"

Jihan: "I haven't played as well as I could have *because you haven't had confidence in me.*"

Me: "It is challenging for me to believe in you when you don't believe in you. I know it seems like I should give you confidence, but don't you understand confidence is something which comes from within? You are a tremendous athlete. Why haven't you heard me when I've told you how great you are?"

Jihan: "I have heard you *but then you don't play me all the time.*"

Me: "I never play anybody 40 minutes and I never will. I do play the players who are playing well the longest. When you are not doing what the team needs, I take you out of the game."

Jihan: "You take me out as soon as I make a mistake *while you let other players stay in the game when they make a mistake.*"

Me: "I don't take you out as soon as you make a mistake. I take you out when you respond poorly to the mistake. What I'm concerned about is your response to the mistake."

Jihan: "*But then you don't put me back in right away.* You put other players right back in the game and I sometimes have to sit for ten minutes before you put me back in."

Me: "Why do you keep comparing yourself to others? This is not about anybody but you. Who else can you control besides yourself?"

Jihan: "Nobody."

Me: "How does it help you to compare yourself to others?"

Jihan: "I just want to know I'm getting my fair share."

Me: "So what exactly is fair?"

Jihan: "I don't know. I just think I should be playing more."

Me: "Were you our leading scorer?"

JIhan: "No, *but I would have been if you would have played me longer and my teammates would have passed me the ball.*"

Me: "Do you understand that you will never get anywhere in life as long as you continue to be a victim?"

Jihan: "I'm not a victim!"

Me: "We all are victims in some way or another. A victim is a person who gives her power away to others. Whenever you blame others or find reasons why you can't do something, you are giving your power away to them. If you tell me, it is up to me for you to become a great player, then I have all your power. I get to determine whether or not you are amazing"

Jihan: "Ouch. You mean all these years I've been giving my power away to others when I blame them for something?"

Me: "Yes. We all do it in a variety of ways, but when we learn to catch ourselves and to stop finding excuses for the way we are, then we start gaining back some of our power."

Jihan: "So when I blame my teammates or you, I am creating excuses rather than finding a way to get it done?"

Me: "Yes. Exactly. Tell me what would happen if you thought I didn't control how well you played."

Jihan: "Then I wouldn't worry about you or what you were thinking. I'd try to find a way to be a better player."

Me: "If I'm not controlling you, how would you see yourself playing?"

Jihan: "I'd be a stud, a three-point shooting, rebounding, low block post-up stud. Heck, I'd be an All-American."

Me: "You have the skill to be an All-American. I've always thought so, and for three years my thoughts haven't mattered. You have to believe that you are an All-American."

Jihan: "Wow. You are right. You've told me forever that I had the tools to be an All-American *but I didn't hear you because you would get on me for playing poor defense or not blocking out.*"

Me: "Do you think I never got on my other All-American players? It is my job to see your potential and to bring it out of you. It is your job to believe in your potential and to hear what I am telling you."

Jihan: "If I start today on working to eliminate my victim mentality I can really be an All-American?"

Me: "Yes. If you see yourself as an All-American and you quit blaming me or your teammates and accept responsibility for your play, you will be an All-American. If you don't accept responsibility for you, you cannot change. You are not ever going to change me or your teammates, but you can change you."

Jihan: "Wow! I never thought of it that way. Thanks Coach."

During Jihan's senior season, she became the team's go-to player averaging a double-double in points and rebounds, piloting us to the conference title and the conference tournament championship. Due to her incredible play, we ended up with a 26-7 record and made it into the national tournament. Jihan became an All-American.

Imagine the experience Jihan could have had if she would have put her victim mentality to rest earlier in her career.

Imagine how you could change your life if you would look for solutions rather than searching for others to blame.

LIMITING BELIEFS

THE UNCONSCIOUS ADOPTION OF BELIEFS

How often have you worked with somebody who didn't know they didn't know? Do you realize that you are one of these people? We only know what we know until we know something more. Socrates said, "The only true wisdom is in knowing that you know nothing." When you know that you know nothing, you are ready to learn everything.

I read a book called *Brave New World* in high school where the government taught people that ignorance was bliss. Life felt better lived in ignorance. If I didn't know something, then I wouldn't feel it. I wouldn't feel the disregard, contempt, jealousy, or loneliness from others. I would be in ignorance heaven.

When I was in my twenties, ignorance sounded like a great proposition to me. But what I didn't know about my limiting beliefs harmed me, because I kept living them. My ignorance failed to save me from pain.

All of us have limiting beliefs. They are the thoughts in our subconscious minds which create how we experience the world. These thoughts are created by past experiences.

WHAT IS A SUBCONSCIOUS BELIEF

What are subconscious beliefs? And how do they develop?

A **belief formed with strong emotions** early in childhood, usually before the age of seven, becomes a subconscious belief. Until this age, we are susceptible to other people's perceptions, because we don't possess a filter in our brains. We accept all words as truth. Our biggest concern is not processing information, but receiving love and security. We are only aware of our own needs and whether those needs are being met.

When I was six, my mother had a meeting at work which went longer than expected. Because she was late, I got hungry and became upset with her. I was unaware of the fallouts of her stressful meeting, or that she had to succumb to the needs of her boss in order to keep her job.

I interpreted I was not receiving my essential needs—safety and food. I decided my mother didn't think I was important enough to be fed when I was hungry and therefore she didn't like me. Later when my mom failed to pick me up at school on time, I knew I was unloved and insignificant. (You can see how this all plays into my limiting belief that nobody liked me.)

This highly charged emotion stayed with me, imbedding itself into my deep subconscious. Although I was not aware of its existence, it became one of the triggers to my irrational emotions.

In my late teens I began dating. When my date showed up late, I immediately assumed he didn't care about me. He was, in my eyes, intentionally being late to prove he was more important than me. I got angry and raw words exploded from my subconscious, blaming and accusing him of being cruel and before I could stop myself, I initiated a fight.

THE FORMING OF BELIEFS

If I could have stepped back from this moment and recognized the trigger of this event, I might have been able to change the relationship pattern and my reactions. However, I didn't realize that my actions were governed by deeply imbedded beliefs. These beliefs, limiting as they were, determined success and failure in all I did.

Any thought which is repeated again and again becomes a belief (which is a fact in your subconscious).

Limiting beliefs usually come from people with whom you have strong connections, like parents, teachers and religious leaders. They can also come from your environment, experiences and traumas.

YOUR PARENTS

You respect and depend on your parents; therefore, you are most susceptible to their beliefs and take on their blueprints about life. If your parents think they have to work hard for money and money is scarce, then you are most likely to have the same financial blueprint and live within the framework of this blueprint. You discover as you age that you make the same amount of money and live the same lifestyle as your parents. Children who come from rich parents expect to make substantial money, because they grow up believing money is available and easy to have. Children who come from poverty remain there, because they learned scarcity.

YOUR TEACHERS

Teachers also have your ear when you are in the early stages of learning. A teacher might inform you that you are a poor speller. Even though you can spell, you think you can't, so you don't spend as much time working on your vocabulary and studying for spelling tests. You create your teacher's expectations, because you fail to put forth the time and effort needed to make yourself a good speller.

YOUR RELIGIOUS LEADERS

Religious leaders are another source for subconscious beliefs because they are valued members of society. It is easy to get hooked on the hypnotic words of the hymnals, communions or prayers. While many of these words are beautiful and soulful, sometimes a well-meaning minister can relate the idea you are not good enough to be God's child, because you are a sinner. The idea that you are not good enough, which is a major limiting belief, can come directly from loving and kind people.

YOUR ENVIRONMENT

Your environment, the culture you grow up in, becomes a major player in your beliefs as well. If you grow up in a community which predominantly shares the same viewpoints, such as an Amish community, it is natural to believe and accept the limiting beliefs about clothes, hair length, farming techniques, and motorized vehicles. While it is easy to view the Amish beliefs as limiting from your distant viewpoint, it may not be as easy to see how you have developed limiting beliefs about religions, race, sexuality or politics from the influence of your own community.

YOUR EXPERIENCES

Your experiences shape your belief system when they have a stimulating emotion attached to them. There is a fine line between experiences and traumas. Experiences, while distressful, can be viewed from the concept of personal growth while traumas tend to be overwhelming and difficult to view from an educational standpoint. Your experience could be failing to make the starting line-up on the basketball team or making an "F" in chemistry. These stressful experiences provided you with lessons on how to overcome perceived failures.

YOUR TRAUMAS

A trauma, on the other hand, is an experience where your pain outweighed any other viewpoint. A trauma could be physical, emotional, mental or spiritual or a combination of the four. Most traumas leave an imprint on all your senses. A trauma could be something as horrific as a traffic accident where somebody was badly maimed or killed or something less horrifying but still excruciating, such as a breakup with a loved one. Either of these incidents could leave you with deeply buried subconscious beliefs which become limiting.

EXAMINING LIFE PATTERNS AND EMOTIONAL TRIGGERS

While I was training for the Olympics, I had several run-ins with my teammates. Since one of my subconscious, limiting beliefs was that nobody liked me, that belief extended to my teammates as well. Imagine the myriad of emotions I went through every time my teammates tried to give me feedback. I took their feedback as personal attacks, and went into anger, frustration, fear, unworthiness, sadness, discouragement, hopelessness, misery and grief.

If I could have tapped into the awareness that what I was hearing was not about me personally, but about my ability on the court, then I could have heard my teammates better, learned quicker, gained confidence, and played with the unity of body and mind.

Your subconscious thoughts occur automatically; they are not readily available for introspection. They are the driver of most of your behaviors even though you don't recognize them. The subconscious mind takes over on the drive to work or the walk around the park. It also sits in the driver's seat in familiar emotional situations. It knows how to operate without your conscious intervention.

The conscious mind is analytical and logical while the subconscious mind is illogical. The conscious mind looks at a problem and tries to solve it with logical steps while the subconscious mind tells you that you are not smart enough to track through the problem-solving steps even though you have graduated from college with two degrees and have 10 years of work experience.

How do you discover these unconscious beliefs if they are buried underneath layers of memories, thought processes and emotions? There are two obvious means of determining limiting beliefs: *(1) recognizing life patterns,* those things which seem to be cyclical, and (2) *paying attention to what triggers you.*

A **life pattern** is something you have established over the years which does not seem to change. For example, you might have a boss who is incompetent, creating five times the work for his team members. You move five states away, change jobs and careers only to discover you attracted the exact characteristics in your new boss. Or you might have had an experience with somebody who is too needy and overtly jealous. You are relieved you had the courage to end the relationship. Two years later in a new relationship, you realize you are dating the same personality with different hair and a shorter nose.

In my athletic career, I had perpetual problems with the teammates I played alongside of and the coaches who trained me. I erroneously thought it was something to do with the OTHER people and if I could remove myself from that team, things would change. Strangely enough, I moved from high school to college, and then from college to the U.S. Olympic Team and still suffered from poor relationships.

Karma was kicking my butt; I was doomed to a life of failed relationships—a pretty dismal feeling since all of life is about relationships. Knowing I possessed the keys to the surrounding events, I would have found life much more enjoyable.

Your life patterns do not resolve themselves by a move or a change; they only resolve themselves through careful analysis of what has been occurring and what you are doing to attract them. Until you recognize the beliefs hidden inside yourself, which cause you to continue repeating your life story, you cannot change.

A **trigger** creates an absurd reaction to an event which should not have caused you to emotionally leap overboard. If an event triggers you to an illogical emotional response and you act like a two-year old, then you know there is a **subconscious LIMITING belief** propelling you toward this response.

Before I spent hours working on my limiting beliefs, I was easily triggered by seemingly innocuous events. A wayward look, a blink of the eye or a simple word transformed me into Lady Frankenstein.

In 2004, I was coaching at the University of Charleston. Dr. Welch, the president of the university, stood outside the locker room after a game we had lost. Dr. Welch regularly visited the locker room after our games to listen to the post game speech. This time, though, the way he stood and the look on his face sent me into a rage. I was smart enough not to take it out on him, but the poor players got blasted for their performance on the court. Even in the middle of my outrageous speech, I knew I was out of balance and bordering on sounding insane, but I couldn't seem to stop myself.

After the president left and I walked outside the locker room, my assistant coach asked me, "What the heck is going on with you?"

"I don't know. I lost control."

"Duh. That was evident. Tomorrow, you might want to apologize to the players. They didn't deserve your wrath."

I honestly didn't know at the time, but later upon reflection, I knew the expression on the president's face reminded me of my father's expressions. My father had high expectations of my performances. After one game in high school where I scored 35 points my father said, "You could have had 42 points if you would have made your free throws."

I'm certain now, after reducing my limiting belief that nobody likes me, that my father was teasing, but I couldn't hear it that way when I was in high school.

My poor players received the offspring of a twenty-year old memory. Most of the time when you react poorly, your reactions are not about what is occurring in the moment. They are a result of all the experiences in your past attached to one of your limiting beliefs.

SUBCONSCIOUS BELIEFS IMPACT OUR RELATIONSHIPS

Life is about relationships—relationships with parents, siblings, teammates, classmates, co-workers, bosses, coaches, and managers. The list goes on forever. You can't live life without managing relationships, unless, of course, you plan on being a hermit or moving to a deserted island.

My subconscious belief that nobody liked me prevented me from enjoying teammates, coaches and bosses. Imagine how my limiting belief played out for people who were around me. How did they feel when I treated them as if they were unlikeable, because that was the way I imagined myself to be? I projected onto other people what I thought about myself. My thoughts were predicated on past experiences.

Relationships are not managed in the here and now; **they are a product of your past histories**, and all the **stories** you've been telling yourself for years. Educate yourself that the behavior of other people is not about you. It is about their own highly charged emotions stored in their subconscious.

Your awareness people are acting from their subconscious minds allows you to reject their words and actions. The truth is their words are *not about you*. If you can separate your feelings of being hurt or injured when somebody else says something cruel to you, you are more likely to get through the moment, forgive the person and live in a happier state of mind.

Let us pretend you are driving down the highway and a car is about to enter the highway from a side entrance. You speed up to allow the car entrance but the driver of the car also speeds up. When he gets beside you, he flips you off and mouths a few choice curse words. You understand this is not about you at all but about his past experiences, shrug your shoulders, and let the moment disappear. If, however, you think his reaction is about you, you question whether you should have sped up or slowed down. You might even feel guilty or shameful.

The last story illustrates how many times a day you can have short-sided relationships with others and take their behavior personally. Now envision how challenging it is to have lengthy conversations without acknowledging the impact of your emotional past.

How people can communicate at all with the emotional trash they have stored in their subconscious minds is beyond comprehension. Imagine a conversation where two people are talking but neither of them is hearing the other one, because they are stuck in their own stories.

> **Jack:** "I'm angry at you for not making it to my birthday party on time." *(He is hurt and injured because his parents were notorious for forgetting him and rarely picked him up from daycare on time.)*
>
> **Molly:** "I didn't mean to get here late. There was a traffic accident." *(Her parents lavished attention on her and rarely were late to anything and when they were, they explained it logically to her with love and affection.)*
>
> **Jack:** "You should have left earlier. You know how long it takes to get here.
>
> **Molly:** "I'm only five minutes late Jack. Five minutes is really nothing."
>
> **Jack:** "Are you saying I'm nothing?"
>
> **Molly:** "No. I didn't say that. I'm just saying five minutes is not a big deal. I'm here now."

Jack: "So you're saying I'm not a big deal—that I'm not that important to you."

Molly: "Jack, why are so angry and hurt? I'm here now."

Jack: "You are never really here even when you are here. Just like now. You don't understand how you've hurt me and act like it is no big deal."

Molly: "It is not a big deal. It was only five minutes. The real issue is that I'm here and I love you. Why can't you understand that my love for you has nothing to do with being five minutes late?"

Jack interprets Molly's lateness as a personal attack on his worthiness. He thinks she intentionally came late despite her assurances she would have been on time without the traffic accident. He cannot hear her, because he is busy *hearing* his parents *tell* him again and again how sorry they were for being late. Their lateness meant he was not important to them and made him feel insignificant and small.

Molly, on the other hand, came from a family who showed their affection physically, always giving her hugs and kisses, and rarely forgot to pick her up on time. On one such occasion when she had to sit on the steps outside the elementary school, her mother drove into the parking lot, jumped out of the car, picked her up, gave her a long bear hug, told her how sorry she was, and then drove her downtown to her favorite ice cream store.

I took most words in my first 40 years of life uttered to me personally. I remained in that hurt place a good portion of every day. My heartache impacted my ability to enjoy life and created havoc in my career as an athlete and a coach.

The question is: Does personally taking another person's past history and pain serve you well?

When you remember we all speak and act from our subconscious minds, and those minds are deeply rooted and automatically controlled, then you can allow other people's words to flow through you. You won't possess the need to trap somebody else's unkind words and receive them personally. You possess enough personal ammunition to beat yourself up for a lifetime. Working on releasing your blame, guilt and unworthiness is enough.

RELEASING THE NEED TO BEAT UP ON YOURSELF

SUFFERING NEVER LESSENS OUR ORIGINAL PAIN

When something doesn't work in your life, how do you beat yourself up? Do you work after hours, eat a double chocolate cheesecake, drink a bottle of wine, or run an extra mile? If you do, you have been taught suffering will lessen your original pain. This is a product of your past.

When I was a teenager I had the habit of berating myself about my mistakes after losing a basketball game. I counted every shot I missed in the game, the defensive errors, and the number of times an opponent scored on me. The loss was my fault. The next day I forced myself to stay in the gym until I paid penance for my mistakes. I worked out until my muscles ached, I couldn't take one more shot, or I had sufficiently paid for my poor performance.

If I would have remained at this novice level of self-abuse maybe I wouldn't have ruined my health, but I didn't remain there. As life presented greater challenges, I found new and more rigorous ways of hurting myself. I learned the art of drinking and suffered horrendous hangovers. I perfected the over-eating syndrome inherited from my mother and gorged food until my stomach hurt. I injured others through careless words and actions resulting in loneliness, and exercised excessive hours wreaking havoc on my body.

None of these things in small doses would have been too damaging, but I needed to suffer so I pushed the limits on everything.

Have you noticed as the challenges in your life escalate, so does your abuse? How often have believed you needed to be punished? Remember when you were a small child and broke your mother's favorite vase, and didn't feel relief until you received a spanking? Most of us were taught we needed to suffer in order to be absolved from our wrongdoings.

Is suffering needed for absolution? O is there another way to look at it?

Eckhart Tolle said, "**Every addiction arises from an unconscious refusal to face and move through your own pain. Every addiction starts with pain and ends with pain. Whatever the substance you are addicted to – alcohol, food, legal or illegal drugs, or a person – you are using something or somebody to cover up your pain.**"

The pain we suffer is by our own hand. We think we can erase one pain by creating another. We believe if we suffer enough, we will be okay.

Where did your idea of suffering originate? Mine came from the Biblical stories I learned in Sunday school and the messages from the preacher. It came from the idea of everlasting hell and being judged. It came from my parents who withheld their love when

I was bad, and from my teachers who sat me in the corner when I couldn't be quiet. It came from watching television, reading books and listening to gossip.

SELF-JUDGMENT LEADS TO PUNISHMENT

My outlook about punishment altered when my understanding grew that suffering separates us from our goodness. We deprive ourselves of feeling good through guilt and shame. We give ourselves no reprieve for learning lessons, believing we have to be perfect the first time. When we yield to the idea of perfection, we prevent ourselves from happiness.

There is nothing right or wrong or good or bad. There are only experiences and opportunities. The guilty cannot feel happy about their journey, because they are too involved in their idea of suffering. We create perceptions about good or bad in our minds. Accepting the belief that everything which happens to us is for our highest good allows us to experience the contrast of life where we are both perfect and imperfect.

The Course in Miracles says, "Guilt feelings are the preservers of time. They induce fears of retaliation or abandonment, and thus ensure that the future will be like the past."

My lessons about suffering didn't come easy. I spent years judging myself, berating myself for all the things I'd done wrong. There was an inventory inside my head listing all the bad and terrible things I had done. When I visited my inventory, I hated myself and the incompleteness viewed there. The inventory caused me to believe I should suffer for my mistreatment of others and my imperfections. Only through punishment could I receive absolution.

I failed to accept the idea of absolute forgiveness. Absolution was too foreign, implying my transgressions could be completely erased. Was forgiveness possible for my lies, deceptions, cruelties, betrayals, treacheries, and infidelities? I couldn't fathom how my offensives could be expunged. Hadn't I done them?

WHAT PART DOES FORGIVENESS PLAY?

"When you forgive, you in no way change the past - but you sure do change the future."
— Bernard Meltzer

Shame and guilt are the two lowest emotions you can retain. Guilt and shame reduce your energy into its lowest vibrational state. To attract what you desire in your life, you must send out high vibrational frequencies. High vibrations attract similar vibrations while low vibrations attract low vibrations. You cannot vibrate in a high intensity when you hold onto a past incident where you desire punishment for yourself or someone else.

You have most likely suffered an incident where somebody hurt you in a way you thought you would never recover. I have a past full of wounds and stories about how people betrayed and abandoned me. Large wounds of fear and misery opened inside me, keeping me vulnerable to new attacks.

I held onto those painful memories, because I believed if I released the memories, then the people who hurt me would not be punished. The pain would be too easily forgotten and the lessons learned would dissipate. Who would be the keeper of those lessons so that they wouldn't happen to me again?

The painful memories fed my anger, shame and guilt. I kept those emotions within me, because I thought I needed them.

Have you ever done that—kept negative emotions because you believed if you let them go, you would lose a part of yourself, or you would forget the lesson and therefore have to repeat it again?

Think about the last time you were sad or angry. Maybe your partner broke up with you and you couldn't seem to get beyond the pain. What you thinking about--things that reinforced your sadness or anger? You listened to the first song you slow danced together. You looked at the photographs of your earliest vacation together in a mountain chateau. Or maybe you ate at his favorite restaurant. You kept the grief running through you by reviewing old memories.

Why did you choose to keep those memories? What was your deeper intent? Were you keeping the memories vivid so you would remember the pain and learn the lesson, or were you keeping them fresh so you could punish yourself or your partner?

When you live in the painful memories of your past, you cannot expect the best for your future. You give the past events more energy by believing you have to hold onto them. The more energy you deposit into your past, the more the past will become your present.

Withholding forgiveness is an attack against yourself. You are locked into a past which cannot be changed, denying yourself the opportunity to move forward. Your unwillingness to forgive binds you to self-hatred, because fear is the opposite of love. Fear of releasing the past is what holds you to your self-hatred. What you deny others, you deny in yourself. The only way to heal the past and thus yourself is forgiveness.

The act of forgiving is not as easy as it seems. Saying "I forgive you" is not enough. The words can be empty if not accompanied by strong emotion. The words are not as crucial as the feeling behind the words. The best way to learn to forgive is to switch your paradigm. Knowing you should forgive is different from the belief in forgiveness.

One method to switch your paradigm is to believe we all come to earth on a journey to learn lessons, moving toward a truer sense of unconditional love. Viewing events as lessons gives us the insight to see that people don't do things to us; they do things FOR us. People are in our lives to help us grow. Only through the contrast of experiences can we gain understanding and compassion. Likewise, what we do to others, we also do for others.

Some people cannot forgive because they believe it is exoneration for behaviors. It is not our duty to punish others. When you believe in cause and effect or you reap what you sow, you know that every person receives what they give. When you give sorrow, you receive sorrow. When you share joy, joy is returned to you. You don't have to see the reciprocal effect as punishment; it is the pathway to learning. In this viewpoint, you can release judgment and your need for punishment while feeling confident justice and peace exist.

What matters is not how you switch your paradigm to find peaceful forgiveness, but that you do switch. Once you disperse with anger, shame and guilt, you live fully in the present. You find the happiness that has eluded you and expect good in every day.

PERFECTIONISM AS ANOTHER FORM OF SUFFERING

Trying to be perfect can be another form of suffering. Perfection is an impossible goal. The gift of life is the contrast, which means there will be failures before the success. You can choose to punish yourself through each of your failures if you believe suffering is necessary for success.

Maybe you are one of the people who believed you had to make straight "A's" in your classes. You studied harder than other students, refraining from movie nights and lounging with friends. You believed the grades were essential to keeping your identity. A "B" on your report card would result in sleepless nights and renouncing even more social events. You never questioned why your grades had to be perfect.

I was one of those straight "A" students. I studied longer and more strenuously than most of my classmates for my grades. When I wrote a paper, I spent weeks preparing for it, doing the research, painstakingly evaluating each word and sentence dissecting them for inadequacies. It was a laborious process but I endured it to feel better about myself, because I needed the "A."

Perhaps the suffering involved for the grade was worth it. I don't know. I needed to feel better about myself and making good grades made me believe I was worthy. The problem was the feeling never lasted long enough. Euphoria came and then in another instant disappeared, forcing me to strive some other way to feel good.

Laziness is not coveted nor is hard work evil. You can enjoy the process, allow for mistakes and love yourself whether you are a straight "A" student or a student who makes a couple of "B's." If you created your "A's" from a place of fun and celebration, enjoying being your best without the need to be perfect, then making the grades were in the spirit of wonder and festivity.

The suffering is the part where we believe we have to be the best or else. Or else what? Or else we are not good enough so we need to suffer. This idea stems from our ego, which means edging goodness out. How can we exude goodness when we believe we do not deserve it?

Even when we succeed, the ego shortens our achievement. The ego rationalizes that although we achieved what we set out to achieve, we still are not worthy.

The ego lessens our achievements by constructing a different story. I lessened my achievements by telling this story:

Even though I was the valedictorian of my university, it didn't mean anything. I graduated from a small university. We didn't have many students and I majored in an easy major, Physical Education and Health. Anybody could have been valedictorian if they would have tried.

Part of living is celebrating our achievements, feeling good about what we've done and who we are. When we fail to do that, we separate ourselves from all that is good. We separate ourselves from our higher power. We keep ourselves locked in the past and reliving our pain. We cannot expect the best nor feel the power of living in our best when we refuse to feel good, because our ego demands more of us. Acceptance of who we are and the belief we are worthy stimulates us to achieve because we want to, not because our ego needs massaging.

THE INNER JUDGE AND BOOK OF LAW

Don Miguel Ruiz in his book, *The Four Agreements*, discusses the judge we have within us. According to Ruiz, we become domesticated by the beliefs of our mothers, fathers, religious leaders and society. We adopt the teachings taught to us and then we build a Book of Law which rules our mind. We build our judgments through our Book of Law and determine whether we should punish or reward ourselves based on how we performed our set of laws.

We learn to judge everything—the dog, the cat, the trees, the flowers, our parents, our experiences and ourselves. We are constantly in a state of judgment and our Inner Judge follows our Book of Law even if the unwritten laws we are obeying don't fit with our inner guidance. Our Inner Judge determines every day how we view ourselves and whether we should feel guilt and shame, or virtuousness and gratification.

We are not aware we follow our Book of Law and that we have the ability to change this book or even throw it away. By following The Inner Judge, we create a mentality of unworthiness. We feel unworthy of our jobs and partners, love and money. It is a vicious cycle and one that is hard to break, because we have been so conditioned to think that we have to be punished when we don't follow the rules we learned.

I was so caught up in my Inner Judge and the Book of Law that I was separated from my inner wisdom. I couldn't touch that part of me which was a higher power nor feel what was right for me, because I was too busy following the rules I had been taught. Somewhere in my diluted thinking, I believed if I was good enough at following the rules, everything I wanted would fall into place.

After I discovered following the rules was not creating my dreams, I faltered. I fell. I plummeted but I never, ever stopped punishing myself. If I wasn't getting what I wanted, I needed to be better, to be more perfect and to rub as much salt in my wounds as possible, so it would be noted I sufficiently punished myself for not being good enough.

What a vicious cycle!

When somebody else doesn't love you, have you chastised yourself and believed it was ALL YOUR FAULT for the breakup?

Or maybe your experience was that your parents didn't love you enough? Maybe they abandoned you emotionally or physically. Did this action cause you to spend time believing you weren't good enough to be loved?

I felt that way more than once. Even now I get triggered with some past experience and fall back into the trap of believing if I had been a better person, I would have been loved. I rehash every moment of the relationship playing the "If-Only Game." Maybe you've played this as well.

- "If only I would have kept the house cleaner."
- "If only I would have been more sensitive."
- "If only I would have been a better lover."
- "If only I would have shared my problems."
- "If only I would have been a better communicator."
- "If only. If only. If only."

How many times have you punished yourself with those words?

Wouldn't it be nice to throw away the belief the relationship would have worked if only you would have been a little bit better? Wouldn't it be nice to stop the punishment of not being good enough and simply believe the relationship wasn't meant to be? Wouldn't it be awesome if you didn't have to assign blame or JUDGE yourself or your significant other?

You can. You have the power to transform how you think.

THE SUFFERING NEVER MADE US BETTER

Most people spend a majority of their lives in punishment for a perceived failure, and the truth is all that suffering did not make them better. They get stuck in this merry-go-round of beliefs thinking they can absolve their inadequacies by sentencing themselves to self-hatred.

Yet when people overeat because they do not like some facet of themselves, do they feel better later? When they fill themselves up with sugar-loaded snacks like ice cream bars from the vending machines, and eat three or four of them in a sitting trying to fill their bodies up with anything besides the doubts rummaging around in their heads, does the sugar high last for more than a few minutes? When they come down from the high, what thoughts kick in?

Nothing positive.

When most people recognize their eating problem, they don't see the underlying problem and try to use willpower to end their issue. Willpower is never enough to stop the underlying causes of ANY problem, which is why it is easy to fail and go back into old habits.

There are three characteristics of the conscious mind you use in your daily challenges: willpower, analytical power and rational power. If you look at the first letter of each of these words, it spells "WAR," which is exactly what it feels like if you are in your conscious mind trying to resolve your issues.

When you battle from your conscious mind, you will discover the battle is harsh, long and fatiguing. There seems no way to win it especially with the Judge and Jury evaluating the battle.

I rubbed salts in my wounds many times in several different ways. Even after awakening, I find myself reverting back to old habits. Today, in fact, I took a nosedive into the cesspool of judgment. I swam in those murky waters, holding my nose but still breathing in the stink for hours.

During the course of changing my career from a basketball coach to a motivational speaker, writer and success coach, I had to learn how to use the computer in a myriad of ways beyond the simple act of typing. When things do not work as they should, when the computer does not play fairly and takes me on some confusing ride, I get frustrated.

The frustration turns into self-abuse. I start with the first step of judgment and before I can reel myself in, I am on a long road of remembering all the reasons why I am not smart enough and don't deserve success. In four hours, I'm in the what-if-down thinking mode and sending myself spiraling down into the depths of misery.

Even when I know this is not healthy, even when I recognize the trap, even when I am fully aware it is my subconscious mind running the show and I can't rage "WAR" against the subconscious mind and win, I try anyway. The more I try to use willpower, rationalization and analytical prowess to beat myself into submission, the wearier I become.

Pretty soon the Judge and Jury have won. I have punished myself by being miserable all day and ruined an opportunity to smile, laugh and find joy.

We cause ourselves to suffer because we think we need to suffer in order to feel better. When you look at those words and read them, they sound pretty pathetic. How can suffering make us feel better? Would we tell somebody with an open wound to rub salt in it and the wound will feel better? Would we tell somebody with a broken leg to run faster on it to make the leg feel better? Would we tell somebody who is agonizing over a decision to hit her head repeatedly against the wall to feel better? No!

Yet, we believe we can make ourselves feel better through our suffering. What if we decided to let the Judge and Jury go? What if we decided to stop the suffering and just love ourselves unconditionally? What would happen?

LETTING GO OF THE JUDGE AND JURY

If you are convinced the Judge and Jury inside your mind aren't serving you well, how do you move forward?

1. When you hear the Judge and Jury ask: Am I willing to let go of this judgment?

2. If the answer is yes, consciously release it. If it helps you to visualize a balloon with the judgment inside of it floating away from you, then do it. You can also create other visualizations to help you visualize the judgment moving away from you.

3. If the answer is no, ask yourself: Why am I unwilling to let this go? Take the time to listen. If an answer comes to you, ask if you are willing to let the answer go. If no answer comes, ask if you can release the judgment.

4. If you continue to receive a no when you ask if you can release the judgment, then release the resistance. By releasing the resistance, you open up the possibility of releasing your next judgment.

5. Practice hearing how you judge yourself. Let the judgment go as soon as you hear it.

6. When you release the judgment say, "I love releasing judgments so I can love myself now and forever."

7. When you judge somebody else, recognize the flaws you are judging in yourself and let them go.

HOW TO MOVE YOURSELF FORWARD
FROM LIMITING BELIEF THINKING

1. How would your life change for the better if you let go of the beliefs that you developed as a child, took back control of your life and changed your current way of thinking? What might be possible?

2. Change Your Thoughts – Change Your Beliefs – Change Your Life.

   In order to replace your limiting beliefs with more positive ones, you need to learn how to observe your thoughts so you can replace negative thoughts with positive ones. When you do this consistently, over time, your internal beliefs start to shift, which will positively impact the results you're experiencing in life.

   a. Identify an area of your life that you have a strong desire to change. It could be anything connected with your health, your wealth, your relationships or a specific situation that you're dealing with right now.

   Write down that area or situation.

   a. Imagine that area of your life or situation and identify any limiting beliefs that might be getting in your way and that you would like to change. Write them down.

   a. Next, identify three negative thoughts that typically come to mind when you think about this area or situation.

   a. Now, go back and next to each thought, write a more positive thought that you can use to replace the negative, limiting thought.

EXAMPLE #1

Area of my life: relationships.

Limiting belief: "Nobody likes me."

Negative thoughts: When I hear myself saying, "I'm uncomfortable meeting new people," I will tell myself to stop.

Positive replacement: Then I will replace those words with, "I know I can say hello, ask questions, and be a good listener."

EXAMPLE #2

Area of my life: health

Limiting belief: "I inherited my family's weight issues."

Negative thoughts: When I hear myself saying, "I'm fat," I will tell myself to stop.

Positive replacement: Then I will replace those words with, "I am responsible for my weight. I can achieve whatever weight I desire."

Practice being aware of these thoughts and listen when you use them. When you hear the negative thought, tell yourself to "STOP" and replace the negative thought with a more pleasing one that you identified. Notice any shifts in how you feel when you replace the negative thought with a more positive one.

Putting it into practice:

    a. What are some ways that you can remind yourself to practice listening to your own thoughts and observing them without judgment so that you can identify which ones serve you and which ones don't?

EXAMPLE: When my body starts to get tense or I recognize anger or jealousy or some other type of negative emotion, I will start to pay attention to my internal words.

CHAPTER EIGHT

LIVING WHO YOU'VE BECOME

WHAT IS AHEAD

"It had long since come to my attention that people of accomplishment rarely sat back and let things happen to them. They went out and happened to things."
— **Leonardo da Vinci**

I was angry, hopeless and on a path of self-destruction in my twenties. People who knew me then would not recognize me today. They might recognize my physical traits, but they wouldn't recognize the inner me.

If you would have told me 20 years ago who I would become, I would have laughed at your folly. I would have viewed you as crazy, insane and unrealistic. If you told me that I would become a great basketball coach and win a national championship, I would have believed you. I would have called you a liar if you told me I would be happy, joyful, optimistic, loving, kind, compassionate, and empathetic.

When I was 28 years old, miserable and despondent, after my Olympic coach sexually harassed me and then the United States Team Handball Federation fired me from my assistant coach's position, I didn't believe there was anything wonderful in this world. I was so disappointed in mankind I thought evil was the prevailing characteristic in people. Love was a myth, some fairy tale printed up in books to give us false hope. Heaven did not exist, but hell was real because I was living it every day.

What happened? I started taking baby steps. Little bitty ones. They didn't even seem to make a difference, but I kept taking them.

This is what happens when you continue on your journey. You take a step and another step and then one day you look up to see how far you've come. The journey won't feel that long or difficult. It will feel right. You will be astonished and yet at the same time unmoved. You will feel as if you've come back to who you were supposed to be. After a couple of years it will be challenging to remember the old you.

The WIN Philosophy and the WINNER Principles will assist you in taking the necessary steps to consistently live in the inner world which will create the outer world you want to experience. Here is the essential point to remember as you embark upon your journey: YOU are the only one responsible for your journey.

You have the ability to make the journey long or short, difficult or easy. You are in charge of the road map, the car and the gas. You will experience shortcuts, detours, unexpected potholes, amazing sights and traffic jams, and **you get to decide how you will receive each of these.** You can make a turn when you don't like where you are going, put the car on cruise control and sit in comfort, or race to the next destination. The key is to know what you want and to have the faith you will get there.

A REVIEW OF THE WIN PHILOSOPHY

Here is a quick review of the WIN Philosophy:

> **W-Widen the Separator Gap.** Be the person who utilizes her special talents to go beyond what most people do. It is the extra effort which tilts the scale to your favor.

> **I-Identify "I AM" as Power Words.** Define yourself as the things you wish to be. Every time you present yourself with power through the use of positive words, you not only identify with those words, you become them.

> **N-Navigate Success** through the belief you are the creator of your experiences. Once you realize how powerful you are, you move through life with greater confidence. This confidence in turn plays a part in the creation of your successes.

I don't have the answers to the formation of your successes but I found the answers to mine. I shared my story with you because other people dared to share their stories with me. Every time I read a book or listened to an audio book, I got a little bit better. These days when I say my daily attitude of gratitude, I include thanks to those people like Dr. Wayne Dyer, Susan Scott, Hal Elrod, Tony Robbins and others who took the time to write their wisdom down on paper. Because they cared enough to share their stories with me, I was able to become a person I love and respect.

When I present seminars or motivational talks, I'm astonished at the number of people who struggle in their lives. They are miserable because they don't know they have a choice to be happy. They don't see how they are in charge of their lives and continue waiting for fate to intervene. While they wait they blame outside events or other people for their misery. Wouldn't it be amazing if they understood by changing themselves, they could change their world?

"The greatest discovery of all time is that a person can change his future by merely changing his attitude."
—Oprah Winfrey

This is my hope for you—that something in my words spark you to personal growth. Maybe I wrote something in a way that allowed you to hear it like you haven't heard it before, or I introduced you to a new way of seeing life. Maybe I reinforced beliefs you already possessed. If I did touch you, please pass it forward to somebody else. Let them borrow your book or buy them a book of their own as a gift. Give them the opportunity to evolve through their personal journey.

THE WINNER PRINCIPLES

I'll never forget an Olympic team handball teammate of mine who taught me a valuable lesson. Cindy, my roommate, had a habit of waking up in the morning, going to the window and looking outside. On the first day we roomed together, she exclaimed, "What a beautiful day it is."

I got up and ran to the window expecting to see a sunny December day. Instead I saw my blue Volkswagen bug almost completely covered in snow. I left the window dejected.

A few days later, Cindy once again exclaimed, "What a beautiful day it is."

Once again I ran to the window expecting to see sunshine. A horrendous sleet storm was bending the trees horizontal to the ground. Disappointed I jumped back into bed pulling the sheets over my head.

After two weeks of watching and listening to Cindy's daily ritual I said, "Cindy, every day you proclaim it is beautiful outside no matter what it looks like. Why do you go to the window to see what it looks like when you already know that you are going to say it is beautiful?"

"To remind myself I get to see what I want."

Cindy had it right. It took me another 20 years to see the beauty in every day.

You can be like Cindy or you can choose to take the long road like I did. I don't advocate going through chronic pain to learn your lessons, but if you think that is what it will take to get you to view the world differently, then I say, "Go for it. It will be worth it in the end."

Along the way to discovering beauty, I learned the WINNER Principles. These principles can be your shortcut to seeing storms in a more positive light.

W-Welcome Your Challenges. Most people get angry when an obstacle gets in the path of what they desire. They view it as problematic, painful, and potentially dangerous. They spend enormous amounts of energy trying to avoid challenges. When you learn that challenges represent opportunity, you move from being fearful to being in charge.

I-Improve Your Communication Skills. How you talk to yourself is critical, because the words you say to yourself become the way you live and how you perceive the world. The language you use internally is the same language you use to communicate to others. When you talk to others in the way you want to be talked to, you increase the chances of a positive relationship.

N-Nourish Yourself. You can get so caught up in the service of others that you forget to nourish yourself. When you suffer the symptoms of burnout, you lack self nourishment. You failed to fuel and balance your mind, body and spirit while creating your life. You are interconnected and when you fail to nourish one portion of your being, your wholeness becomes split. This split can be reconnected by establishing habits which nourish each interdependent part of you.

N-Nurture Your Relationships. Your relationships determine your family life, your career advancements and your social engagements. Your first important relationship is with yourself, learning to love yourself unconditionally. From self-love you can then interact with other people by reflecting your love onto them. When you love others where they are at in their lives, allowing them to be who they are without judgment, you give to them a precious gift, and in return, they will present you with multiple gifts.

E-Expect the Best. You become who you believe you are. The more you see the best in yourself, the more you experience success. You don't get what you want; you get who you are. By aligning yourself with the best possible outcome and having the faith that you deserve the best, you become your desires. You are your own worst enemy, but you can also be your best ally. The difference between being your enemy or your ally is expectations. Expectations create your future just as they determined your past.

R-Recover From Your Past. You use the past as a gauge to prove what you can or cannot do. The past is the past and it can be repeated or you can choose to let it go. You possess the power to become who you want to be no matter who you were or what you've done. By letting go of your judgment, by releasing the need to be right, and disengaging from the victim mentality, you can move forward rather than exist in the past.

I would love to help you evolve. You can reach me by email at **coachwinnspeaks@gmail.com** or through my website **www.coachwinnspeaks.com**. Please share your successes with me. Let me know how you've evolved and who you've become through the WIN philosophy and WINNER Principles.

No one else can give to you as much as you need to give to yourself. The only person who determines your life is YOU. You are the ultimate creator.

REFERENCES

WORKS CITED

Cialdini, Robert. Influence: The Psychology of Persuasion. New York: HarperCollins, 2009.

Covey, Stephen. The Seven Habits of Highly Effective People: Powerful Lessons in Personal Change. New York: Simon and Schuster, 1989.

Dwoskin, Hale. The Sedona Method: Your Key To Lasting Happiness, Success, Peace and Emotional Well-being. Sedona, AZ: Sedona Press, 2007.

Elrod, Hal. The Miracles Morning: The Not-So-Obvious Secret Guaranteed to Transform Your Life Before 8 AM. Hal Elrod International, 2012.

Foundation for Inner Peace. A Course in Miracles. Mill Valley, CA: Foundation for Inner Peace, 1976.

Georgia Career Information Center. 2006. "From High School to Pro – How Many Will Go?" Georgia Career Information Center (Online). http://freedom.mysdhc.org/guidance/information/From%20High%20School%20to%20Pro%20Statistics.pdf

Gephert, Nadja. (June 17, 2011). "Three Steps to Unlock the Power of Bad Feelings." Psychology Today (online).

Hill, Napoleon. Think and Grow Rich. Hollywood, FL: Simon & Brown, 2010 (First copyright 1937).

Lally, P., van Iaarsveld, C.H.M., Potss, H.W.W. and Wardle, J. (2010), "How are habits formed: Modelling habit formation in the real world." Eur. J. Soc. Psychol. 40:998-1009.

Maraboli, Steve. Unapologetically You: Reflections on Life and Human Experience. Port Washington, NY: A Better Today Publishing, 2013.

Ratey, John J, MD. A User's Guide to the Brain: Perception, Attention and the Four Theatres of the Brain. New York: Vintage Books, 2001.

Rubin, Gretchen. The Happiness Project: Or Why I Spent a Year Trying to Sing in the Morning, Clean My Closets, Fight Right, Read Aristotle, and Generally Have More Fun. New York, HarperCollins, 2009

Ruiz, Don Miguel. The Four Agreements: A Practical Guide to Personal Freedom (A Toltec Wisdom Book). San Rafael, CA: Amber-Allen Publishing, Inc., 2012.

Sapolsky, Robert. PhD. Why Zebras Don't Get Ulcers. New York: Henry and Holt Company, 2004.

Scott, Susan. Fierce Conversations: Achieving Success at Work & in Life, One Conversation at a Time. New York: Berkley Books, 2002.

Walsch, Neal Donald. Conversations with God, An Uncommon Dialogue, Vol.1. New York: Putnam Adult, 1996.

ACKNOWLEDGMENTS

There are not enough pages in a book to acknowledge all the people who have made a difference in my life. Some of you have written books, produced pod-casts, webinars or even television shows. Other have hugged me, supported me and loved me through challenges. To all of you, I send blessings and hugs.

Pam Winn
Darlene Chandler
Dr. Clarence Winn
Lauretta Yantis
Reita Clanton
Lynne Fitzgerald
Dr. Danny Brassell
Kathryn Roberts
James Malinchak
LaVonna Roth
Lila Larson
Kevin Clayson
Gary Barnes
Dr. Bren Stevens
Dr. Edward Welch
Oprah Winfrey
Dr. Wayne Dyer
Ellen DeGeneres
Eric Lambert
Cynthia Stinger
MaryPhyl Dwight
Forbes Riley
John Assaraf

Brian Tracy
Stephanie Fofonoff
Brene' Brown
Jane Krizek
David Otey
Laura
Morledge Anderson
Barb Clementi
Ashley Warren
Carlos Lopez
Trisha Glen
Dee Miller
Hillary Summers
Billings
Chamber of Commerce
Deborah
"Atianne" Wilson
Cary Veis
Stacy Birnbach
The Donaldson Family
Zig Ziglar
Jim Rohn
Donnette Roberts

Izabela Lundberg

Don Miguel Ruiz

John Maxwell

Deepak Chopra

Byron Katie

Chris Moat

Derek Dukes

MSU-Northern

Rachel Pike

MOTIVATE AND INSPIRE OTHERS!
Share this Book!

Each one of us has a WINNER within us. Your winner might show up in different ways-emotional, social or spiritual intelligence, athleticism, or a host of other talents. What matters is that you BELIEVE you are a winner and then take the steps necessary to become one. By reading this book, you've committed to unleashing even more of your inner winner. Imagine sharing this book with those you love and how you can help them see the winner they were born to be.

Retail $24.95
Special Quantity Discounts

5-20 Books	$21.95
21-99 Books	$18.95
100-499 Books	$15.95
500-999 Books	$10.95
1,000+ Books	$8.95